The Rules in Practice

Fifth Edition

Bryan Willis

Regular updates to this book can be found on our website

www.fernhurstbooks.co.uk

Copyright © Bryan Willis 2001

First published 2001 by
Fernhurst Books,
Duke's Path, High Street, Arundel,
West Sussex, BN18 9AJ, UK

Earlier editions published in 1985, 1989, 1993
and 1997

British Library Cataloguing in Publication Data.
A catalogue record for this book is available
from the British Library.

ISBN 1 898660 77 8

This fifth edition has been updated to comply
with the new rules, approved at the International
Sailing Federation conference in November
2000, and becoming effective in April 2001.

Printed in Great Britain by Ebenezer Baylis

Artwork by Creative Byte

Cover design by Simon Balley

Cover photo by Rick Tomlinson

Drawings from photos by Shelley Baxter

Edited by Tim Davison

**For a free, full-colour brochure
write, phone, fax or email us:**

Fernhurst Books, Duke's Path,
High Street, Arundel, West Sussex
BN18 9AJ, United Kingdom.

Phone: 01903 882277
Fax: 01903 882715
Email: sales@fernhurstbooks.co.uk
Website: www.fernhurstbooks.co.uk

Contents

Introduction 6

The rule Changes 7

1   The Basics 9

2   Before the Preparatory Signal 15

3   In the Preparatory Period 16

4   The Start 21

5   The Gate Start 28

6   On the Beat 29

7   Rounding the Windward Mark 38

8   On the Reach 49

9   Rounding the Wing Mark 57

10 Rounding the Leeward Mark from the Reach 62

11 On the Run 64

12 Rounding the Leeward Mark from the Run 70

13 The Finish 74

14 Means of Propulsion 77

15 Taking a Penalty 78

16 Protesting 80

17 Requesting Redress & Appealing 83

The Racing Rules of Sailing for 2001 - 2004

Introduction 85

Basic Principle 85

Part 1   Fundamental Rules 85

Part 2   When Boats Meet 85

Part 3   Conduct of a Race 86

Part 4   Other Requirements When Racing 88
Part 5   Protests, Redress, Hearings, Misconduct & Appeals 89
Part 6   Entry and Qualification 91
Part 7   Race Organization 91

Appendices, Section I

A   Scoring 92
B   Sailboard Racing Rules 93
C   Match Racing Rules 93
D   Team Racing Rules 96
E   Radio-Controlled Boat Racing Rules 97
F   Appeals Procedures 99
G   Identification on Sails 99
H   Weighing Clothing and Equipment 100
J   Notice of Race and Sailing Instructions 100
N   Immediate Penalties for Breaking Rule 42 102

Appendices, Section II

1   ISAF Advertising Code 102
2   ISAF Eligibility Code 104
3   ISAF Anti-Doping Code 105

Index 108
Definitions 110
Race Signals 111

Introduction

This book is primarily for competitive sailors who race in dinghies and keelboats. The Racing rules of Sailing apply to all forms of sailboat racing, though there are some variations for sailboards, match racing, team racing, radio controlled boat racing, etc. I have aimed to examine about one hundred situations that are a regular feature of both championship and club racing. Unlike most other books on the racing rules, I look at these situations from the point of view of you, the helmsman. Placing you in each of the boats involved in turn, I explain your rights and your obligations. Being confident about this knowledge not only means you avoid breaking a rule and have to take a penalty, but that you can concentrate on exploiting the situation to gain boat lengths over your immediate rivals.

It is popular misconception that to be good at boat-to-boat tactics you need to know the rules. The rules, the rule numbers, the case law - all that can be sorted out before the start of the hearing if there is a protest. What you need to know out there on the water are your rights and your obligations; what you are allowed to do, and what you must and mustn't do. You need to know them automatically and subconsciously, so that you can concentrate on manoeuvring and sailing fast, to exploit the situation to the full. It is just as satisfying to come away from a mark in the lead having approached it in second place as it is to spend twenty minutes overhauling your rival with superior boatspeed. There is no satisfaction in sailing faster than everyone else on a leg if you throw away your position through being uncertain about your rights and obligations when you come to round the mark.

The book should also be useful in the preparation of a protest, or the defence should you be protested. Each situation shows the critical questions which have to be considered and which will determine the 'facts found' and, therefore, the result of the hearing.

Because almost all the rules of racing apply to the boats rather than to the people sailing them, most books on the rules, and indeed the rules themselves, use the pronoun 'she'. Since I aim to look at situations from the point of view of you, the helmsman, I use the pronoun 'you'; and for the helmsman of the other boat 'he' and 'him'*. However, bear in mind that it is what the boat does that matters. The intentions of the people sailing the boats are irrelevant (provided that they are not malicious). Even most hails are irrelevant. What each boat actually does is usually all that counts.

This fifth edition has been updated to comply with the changes introduced in 2001 by the ISAF (the International Sailing Federation, formerly the International Yacht Racing Union).

Publisher's note: 'or she' is implied throughout.

The Rule Changes

Every four years the rules are updated. In 1997 there was a major revision of rules and terminology. The old 'Yacht Racing Rules' became the new simplified 'Racing Rules of Sailing'. A leeward boat was no longer allowed to 'luff as she pleased' and everyone became required to try to avoid collisions. In the last edition of this book I outlined the major changes to help experienced sailors through the transition. Sailors new to racing don't need to know about changes.

In this rules revision, there were few significant changes between the 1997-2000 rules and the 2001-2004 rules.

The only changes that will affect almost all sailors are as follows.

- The standard signalling system for starting races has changed. 'System 1' with a class flag at ten minutes before the start, a P flag at five, and both dropped at the start, and 'System 2' with Yellow, Blue, and Red signals going up at the 10, 5 and start, and staying up for 4 minutes, have been replaced with a single system. The warning signal is now the class flag which goes up at five minutes before the start, the preparatory signal is usually the P flag and goes up 4 minutes before the start and comes down one minute before the start. The class flag comes down at the start. If the race committee decides to apply a penalty system (often necessary with large competitive fleets) then the P flag is replaced with an I, Z, or black flag.

- Dinghies don't need to carry a protest flag. More exactly, any boat under 6 metres doesn't need to display a flag when protesting whether or not it has a keel. (The hail of 'protest' is still essential.)

Other changes

- After the starting signal, when boats are about to cross each other on opposite tacks, and the port-tack boat is keeping clear of a starboard-tack boat, the starboard-tack boat must not change course if as a result the port-tack boat would immediately need to change course to continue keeping clear. This is a new obligation for the right-of-way boat. The broader obligation on a right-of-way boat to 'give room' when changing course remains (except when sailing a proper course to round a mark - see new rule 18.2(d)). (Rule 16.2 was added in November 1999 and changed in November 2000.)

- The 'slam dunk': Under the 1997-2000 rules, when A crossed ahead of B and tacked, and before the tack was complete B became overlapped within two of her hull lengths to leeward of A, B could not sail above her proper course while they remain overlapped. Under the new rules, B retains her rights to sail above her proper course. (Rule 17.1)

- The mark-rounding rules have been improved. Generally, if you are clear ahead, or overlapped inside, as you reach the two hull-length 'zone' you can at least sail your proper course round the mark even if the overlap situation changes within the zone. (Rule 18)

- When boats are overlapped at a mark and the inside boat has right-of-way, in addition to keeping clear (the only obligation under the old rule), the outside boat must now also give room. (Rule 18.2(a))

- If I and O are overlapped at the two-length zone and the overlap is then broken, the boat that was outside (O) must continue to give I room. If O becomes clear astern or overlapped inside I, O is not entitled to room and must keep clear. (Rule 18.2(b))

- When A is clear ahead of B when they reach the zone, B must thereafter keep clear. If B becomes overlapped on the outside B must also give room, and if B becomes overlapped on the inside B is not entitled to room. (Rule 18.2C)

- When a right-of-way boat is changing course to round or pass a mark, she is no longer required to 'give room' to the other boat. 'Course' always means 'heading' in the racing rules. This change removes the anomaly under the old rules in which the right-of-way boat was prevented from sailing her proper course around a mark because of her obligation to give room to the give-way boat which was sailing a course which allowed the right-of-way boat to sail only a straight-line course. (Rule 18.2(d))

- If boats are approaching a windward mark on opposite tacks, and boat O completes a tack within the zone when boat I is fetching the mark, and I becomes overlapped inside O, then O must give room to I. Under the old rules O merely had to keep clear. (Rule 18.3)

- When an inside overlapped right-of-way boat must gybe at a mark or obstruction to sail her proper course, the obligation to sail no farther from the mark or obstruction than needed to sail that course, now ends when she gybes. (Rule 18.4)

- While boats are passing a continuing obstruction, a boat clear astern that obtains an inside overlap is entitled to room to pass between the other boat and the obstruction only if at the moment the overlap begins there is room to do so. If there is not, she is not entitled to room and shall keep clear. Under the old rule a boat would break the rule (and be subject to penalty) if she obtained an overlap when there wasn't room to pass. Now she is simply not entitled to room. (Rule 18.5)

- The old rules could be interpreted such that a boat sailing to the pre-start side of the line to ensure she was not on the wrong side of the line at the start, or in the final minute of a 'round the ends' start, had to keep clear of other boats. The new rules say that she has to keep clear only after her starting signal. (Rule 20)

- If you are wrongfully compelled to touch a mark, you no longer have to protest. You can just sail on. If there is a protest (for example by you, or by the boat that wrongfully compelled you, or by a third boat) then provided the protest committee is satisfied that as a consequence of another boat breaking a rule you were compelled to touch the mark, you will be exonerated. (Rule 31.3 has been deleted. See also rules 64.1(b) and 31.1)

- It is now clear that a boat doesn't break a rule when a crew member falls overboard accidentally or leaves the boat to swim, provided they are back on board before the boat continues in the race. (Rule 47.2)

- A protest committee that receives a report of an incident that may have resulted in serious damage or injury may protest any boat involved, even if there was no other protest or there was an invalid protest. (Rule 60.4)

- Other than at a world or continental championships, an Organising Authority may still reject or cancel the entry of a boat or exclude a competitor, but now an entry cannot be rejected because of 'advertising' (unless the boat or competitor is not complying with the ISAF Advertising Code). The code itself is no longer an appendix of the rulebook. (Rule 76.1)

1 The Basics

There are certain obligations which you have all the time, so I will state them here and not repeat them in the rest of the book.

You must sail fairly. Sailboat racing is the greatest sport. Generally, we don't have umpires or judges or referees; we police ourselves. Cheats can spoil any sport, and currently our sport is free of cheats (unlike some other sports). We all need to work to keep it that way. So the rules require that as a sailor you conduct yourself in a sportsmanlike manner at all times, and don't bring the sport into disrepute. This principle applies as much to club racing as it does to championships. Trying to gain an advantage by deliberately infringing a rule or lying at a protest hearing is cheating and the penalties for cheating can be severe. In recent years, competitors found guilty of cheating have been disqualified from entire championships and some have been banned by their national authorities or by the International Sailing Federation from taking part in competitive sailing for a year or more (Basic Principle: 'Sportsmanship and the Rules' & Rule 69 'Allegations of Gross Misconduct').

You must help anyone you see in danger. If you lose a position while acting the hero, you will be entitled to redress. (Rule 1 'Helping those in danger', Rule 60.1(b) 'Right to ... Request Redress', Rule 62.1(c) 'Redress').

When you break a rule of Part 2 ('When Boats Meet'), and the other party is clearly aggrieved, you must promptly do your penalty turns. To continue to race without taking a penalty knowing you have broken a rule, hoping perhaps that no one will protest, or through your courtroom skills you might outwit a protestor in the protest room, is an infringement of the Basic Principle 'Sportsmanship and the Rules'.

Even when you have right-of-way or the right to room, you must try to avoid contact. If you don't, and there is damage, you must take a penalty. If there is serious damage the penalty option is not open to you and you must retire. (Rule 14 'Avoiding Contact', Rule 44.1 'Taking a Penalty').

Whether or not you may display advertising on your hull or sails will usually depend on what your class association has decided at an AGM. If you go to an open regatta, the organisers might require you to put advertising (which they will supply) on the forward part of your hull. You may advertise (if it's not too rude!) as much as you like on clothing. (Rule 79 'Advertising' and the ISAF Advertising Code).

I emphasise that these principles apply all the time, and to every situation described in this book.

If you are involved in an incident during a race and you believe another boat (or boats) broke a rule, you must hail 'protest' at the first reasonable opportunity. In addition, if your hull is 6 metres long or more, you need to display a protest flag and keep it displayed until the end of the race.

There are a few terms and definitions that you need to know before we start.

International Sailing Federation (ISAF)

The international governing body that publishes the racing rules and, for guidance on their interpretation, publishes cases that have been decided and submitted by national authorities. (The A in ISAF is there because the International Softball Federation seized the initials ISF before the ISAF changed its name in September 1996 from the International Yacht Racing Union.)

National Authority

Every sailing nation has a national body to administer sailing on waters within its jurisdiction. In Great Britain this is the Royal Yachting Association, in the United States it is the US Sailing Association, in Australia the Australian Yachting Federation, in New Zealand the NZ Yachting Federation, and so on.

Organising Authority

The body which decides to hold an event and arranges the venue. The organising authority might be a club, a class association or a national authority, or a combination of these. At least one of its constituents must be affiliated to the national authority. Sailing clubs are Organising Authorities for their club racing. They might be affiliated to their national authorities through state or district organisations that are in turn affiliated to the national authority. An international class association usually joins with a club to form the Organising Authority to run a world championship. The Organising Authority must appoint a race committee. At a principal event (such as an open regatta or a national champion-ship) it may also appoint a jury, or at an international event, an international jury.

Race committee

The race committee, appointed by the Organising Authority, is responsible for producing sailing instructions, organising the racing and publishing the results. When no jury or international jury has been appointed, the race committee must form or appoint a protest committee when one is needed.

Protest committee

A protest committee is appointed by the race committee when neither a jury nor an international jury has been appointed by the organising authority, to hear protests and requests for redress. The term 'protest committee' is some-times used to describe a jury or international jury when it hears protests and requests for redress.

Jury

A committee separate from and independent of the race committee, appointed by the organising authority at a major event. In addition to hearing protests and requests for redress, its members often go afloat during dinghy regattas to encourage rule compliance and implement the 'yellow flag protest system' for penalising boats breaking Rule 42 'Propulsion'.

International jury

Appointed by the organising authority, its role is the same as that of a jury. However, its membership is made up of people of different nationalities, the majority of whom must be international judges (appointed by the ISAF). Provided that it conducts itself in accordance with the procedures described in Appendix Q, its decisions are not open to appeal.

Appeal authority

Each national authority appoints a committee to hear appeals by competitors (and race committees) against decisions of protest committees and juries (but not International

Juries). For example, in the United Kingdom, the Royal Yachting Association's Racing Rules Committee hears appeals; in the United States of America, appeals are decided by District Appeals Committees, and some are subsequently referred to the United States Sailing Association's Appeals Committee. There is no higher appeal authority than the one provided by the national authority having jurisdiction over the event. The Inter-national Sailing Federation does not hear appeals.

Obstruction

'An obstruction is an object that a boat could not pass without changing course substantially, if she were sailing directly towards it and one of her hull lengths from it. An object that can be safely passed on only one side and an area so designated by the sailing instructions are also obstructions. However, a boat racing is not an obstruction to other boats unless they are required to keep clear of her, give her room or, if Rule 21 applies, avoid her.' The committee boat, a rescue boat, a capsized dinghy, the shore, perceived underwater dangers or shallows, and a boat on starboard-tack on a collision course in relation to a port-tack boat are all obstructions. In the case of the committee boat it will also be a mark when it is specified as being at one end of the starting or finish line. A half-metre diameter inflatable buoy is not an obstruction whether or not it is a mark.

Keeping clear (see diagram opposite)

'One boat keeps clear of another if the other can sail her course with no need to take avoiding action and, when the boats are overlapped on the same tack, if the leeward boat could change course in both directions without immediately making contact with the windward boat.' In dinghies in a Force 2 on flat water, 'keeping clear' can be synonymous with 'avoiding a collision' (for example in a 'port and starboard' encounter on a beat in which the port-tack boat ducks under the stern of the starboard-tack boat), but were they to be large keelboats in a Force 6 and a heavy sea, an obligation on you to 'keep clear' might mean leaving a boat-length or more between you and the right-of-way boat. Furthermore, when you are the give-way boat, you must not intimidate the right-of-way boat such that he thinks there is going to be a collision and is forced to take avoiding action. So even in fairly light conditions it's as well to look under the boom and give him a smile, so he knows you are paying attention, before diving under his stern and missing him by a millimetre.

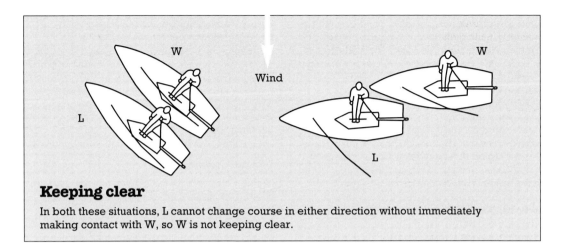

Keeping clear

In both these situations, L cannot change course in either direction without immediately making contact with W, so W is not keeping clear.

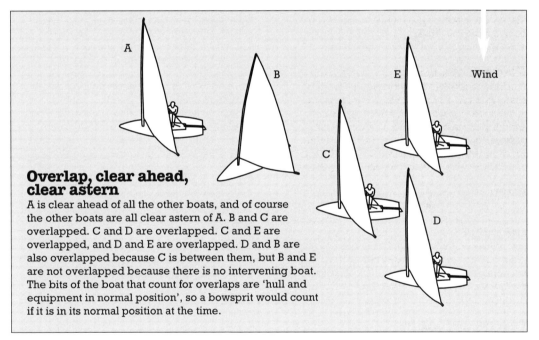

Overlap, clear ahead, clear astern

A is clear ahead of all the other boats, and of course the other boats are all clear astern of A. B and C are overlapped. C and D are overlapped. C and E are overlapped, and D and E are overlapped. D and B are also overlapped because C is between them, but B and E are not overlapped because there is no intervening boat. The bits of the boat that count for overlaps are 'hull and equipment in normal position', so a bowsprit would count if it is in its normal position at the time.

Hailing

A hail is a meaningful word or string of words capable of being heard in the prevailing conditions by the occupants of the boat to which it is addressed. (This is not a defined term - but it's a useful definition, supported by appeal cases.)

You are never actually **required** to make a hail, but when you want to protest you have to hail 'protest' at the first reasonable opportunity; and when you're approaching an obstruction close-hauled and want a boat to give you room to tack, he is not required to take any action until you hail.

When the other boat hails you, you don't always have to respond. You should remember the situations when you must respond to a hail from the other boat:

- When he hails for room to tack because he's close-hauled approaching an obstruction.

- When, after you have hailed for room to tack because you are close-hauled and need room to tack at an obstruction, he replies 'you tack'.

Some other hails might help to establish

something, such as the right to room at a mark, or warn a port-tack boat of your presence ('Starboard!') but these hails in themselves place no obligation on anyone to do anything, so they have no real relevance.

When a hail from you means the other boat must respond, there is the obvious obligation on you not to make the hail unless the conditions exist for you to make the hail. For example, when you are close-hailed and believe you are approaching shallow water and cannot tack without the possibility of colliding with a boat astern or to windward, you may of course hail for room to tack, but you have no right to hail merely for tactical reasons.

Layline

The course on which your boat, sailing close-hauled on starboard tack, can just lay a windward mark which is to be rounded to port is the starboard-tack layline for that mark, and the most windward line on which you would approach the mark on port tack is the port-tack layline. High performance boats with powerful asymmetric spinnakers or gennakers go much faster down-wind by reaching and gybing, so a leeward mark has laylines which are the proper courses for the boats approaching on each tack. Tidal streams distort laylines; a stream going with the wind makes the angle between the windward mark port and starboard laylines wider, and the leeward mark laylines narrower. As the wind gets lighter, the angle between the leeward mark laylines for high-performance boats with asymmetric spinnakers or gennakers gets dramatically wider. A cross-course tidal stream swings the laylines towards the tide. 'Layline' is not a term used in the rulebook, but the term 'proper course' is, and laylines are the extremes of proper courses, so need to be understood. And of course an under-standing of laylines is essential for all tacticians.

Luffing rights

This term is not used in the rulebook either, but sailors often use it, and so I use it in this book. You have 'luffing rights' when you have the right to sail higher than your proper course, forcing a boat to windward of you to change course to keep clear. Provided you didn't establish the overlap to leeward of the windward boat, from astern and within two lengths, a leeward boat has luffing rights, and may luff right up to head-to-wind, but she must give the windward boat room to keep clear. (Rules 11 and 16)

Before the starting signal there is no 'proper course' so any leeward boat may luff up to head-to-wind no matter how the overlap was established (provided the windward boat can keep clear). But at the moment the starting signal is made, any leeward boat that established the overlap from clear astern within two lengths must bear away to close-hauled (if the first leg is a beat) unless as a result of sailing above close-hauled she promptly sails astern of the other boat (which allows her to tack out of the windward boat's wind-shadow). (Rules 11, 16 and 17.1)

Proper course (see diagram opposite)

A proper course is 'A course a boat would sail to finish as soon as possible in the absence of the other boats referred to in the rule using the term. A boat has no proper course before her starting signal.' You're never required to sail a proper course, but there are some situations in which you mustn't sail above your proper course, and others in which you mustn't sail below your proper course, so you need to know what a proper course is.

Sailing instructions

The race committee must produce sailing instructions and make them available to you in time for you to read them before the race or series. They contain two types of information:

• The intentions of the race committee; these instructions contain the word 'will'. For example, 'All marks will be large orange spheres'.

• The obligations of boats and individual competitors; these instruction contain the word 'shall'. For example, 'All marks shall be rounded to port'.

The two types of instructions are mixed together because they are ordered chronologically.

It is imperative that you read the sailing instructions carefully before a race or series. I doubt if there is a champion who has not at some time lost an important race or series through failing to read or remember some particular sailing instruction.

The penalty for not complying with a sailing instruction describing a boat's obligation is disqualification from a race (unless some other penalty is specified), but the penalty can usually be applied only after a hearing.

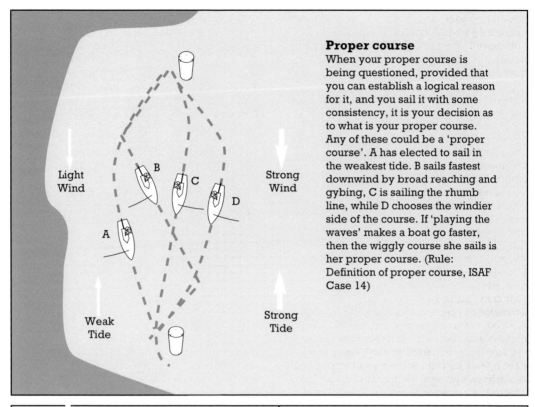

Proper course

When your proper course is being questioned, provided that you can establish a logical reason for it, and you sail it with some consistency, it is your decision as to what is your proper course. Any of these could be a 'proper course'. A has elected to sail in the weakest tide. B sails fastest downwind by broad reaching and gybing, C is sailing the rhumb line, while D chooses the windier side of the course. If 'playing the waves' makes a boat go faster, then the wiggly course she sails is her proper course. (Rule: Definition of proper course, ISAF Case 14)

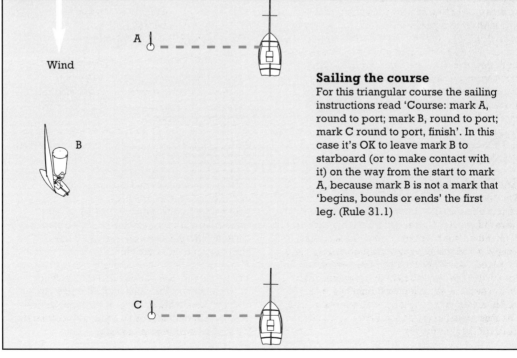

Sailing the course

For this triangular course the sailing instructions read 'Course: mark A, round to port; mark B, round to port; mark C round to port, finish'. In this case it's OK to leave mark B to starboard (or to make contact with it) on the way from the start to mark A, because mark B is not a mark that 'begins, bounds or ends' the first leg. (Rule 31.1)

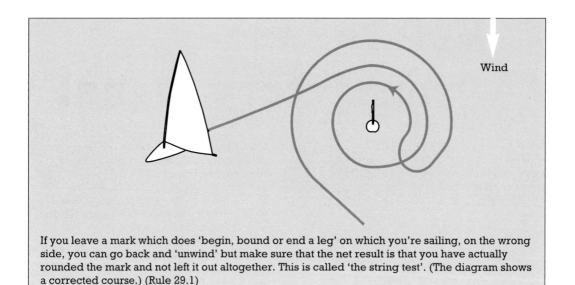

If you leave a mark which does 'begin, bound or end a leg' on which you're sailing, on the wrong side, you can go back and 'unwind' but make sure that the net result is that you have actually rounded the mark and not left it out altogether. This is called 'the string test'. (The diagram shows a corrected course.) (Rule 29.1)

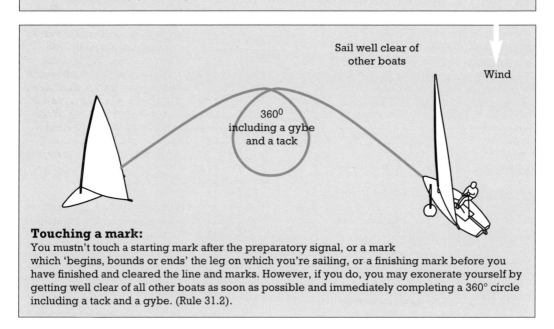

Touching a mark:
You mustn't touch a starting mark after the preparatory signal, or a mark which 'begins, bounds or ends' the leg on which you're sailing, or a finishing mark before you have finished and cleared the line and marks. However, if you do, you may exonerate yourself by getting well clear of all other boats as soon as possible and immediately completing a 360° circle including a tack and a gybe. (Rule 31.2).

No such penalty can be applied to the race committee when it does not carry out its own intentions specified in the sailing instructions, or it fails to comply with a rule which governs its conduct (Parts 3 and 7 of the Rules). What penalty could be imposed without adversely affecting innocent competitors? (The committee could be hung, drawn and quartered, but who would run the next race?) You should bear in mind that the race committee is invariably trying to do a good job of running the races. If the committee makes

an error or an omission and this affects your finishing position in the race or series (and only if it affects your finishing position, and through no fault of your own), then you can ask for 'redress'. A good race committee, realising its erroneous action has affected a boat's finishing position, will itself initiate a redress hearing. Chapter 17 deals with redress hearings. One of the most common errors is to write confusing or ambiguous sailing instructions about the course, resulting in some boats sailing one course and some sailing another.

2 Before the Preparatory Signal

Before going afloat you usually have to enter, register or 'sign on' and may be required to show your measurement certificate. These requirements will be described in the sailing instructions.

To the water! Although the 'when boats meet' rules apply in the same way before as they do after the preparatory signal, there is no penalty for breaking a rule of Part 2 ('when boats meet') unless you interfere with a boat that is racing. (Rule 22.1)

If you break a rule of Part 2 before the preparatory signal, you do not need to retire or take a penalty (but you or your insurance company might have to pay for the damage if there is any).

The rules or sailing instructions (including all of Part 4 of the rules) requiring you to do something 'whilst racing' don't apply before the preparatory signal either, because you're not racing till the preparatory signal.

However, you can be disqualified (after a protest and a hearing) for breaking some other sailing instruction, even if you're not racing when the infringement occurs.

If your boat is damaged in a collision and it wasn't your fault, it is useful to have a protest form showing that the hearing found the other boat to be in the wrong. So it's worth remembering that you can protest another boat for breaking a rule of Part 2 (the 'when boats meet' rules) before the preparatory signal or after the finish, and if the other boat does not accept that he broke a rule, the race committee must hear the protest if it is valid, even though no penalty is applied to the other boat. You must hail 'Protest', and lodge the written protest within the time limit.

The standard signalling system for starting a race is a series of visual signals (usually flags) each accompanied by a sound signal. The sequence begins with the 'Warning Signal' (usually your class flag) at five minutes before the start. One minute later is the 'Preparatory Signal' signalling the beginning of the four-minute 'preparatory period' in which boats are 'racing' (even though they are not going anywhere) and a boat breaking a rule of Part 2 must take an exonerating turns penalty. The visual signal is usually the code flag 'P' (blue with a white square in the middle) which means there will be no 'starting penalty'. At one minute before the start, the preparatory flag is lowered, and at the start the class flag is lowered. When there is a lot of boats all eager to get a good start, the race committee can substitute the 'P' flag with an 'I', a 'Z' or a 'black flag' to bring into effect a penalty system during the final minute. (Rules 26 and 30)

The sailing instructions might vary the standard signalling system. For example, the Warning Signal might be 10 minutes before the start instead of the standard five.

You should be near the committee boat and watching it closely when the Preparatory Signal is made so that you can set your watch. This is especially important in a big fleet where you might start some distance from the committee boat and it is often impossible to see the visual starting signal or hear the 'gun' (and remember the sound takes a while to travel the length of a long starting line).

3 In the Preparatory Period

This section covers the period from the preparatory signal to the time at which boats are approaching the line to start.

At the moment of the preparatory signal your boat must be afloat and off moorings and thereafter not be hauled out or 'made fast' (tied up) except to bail or reef or make repairs, or swim. However, you may anchor at any time, but you must recover your anchor if possible before proceeding. Your crew may stand on the bottom (in shallow water of course) to hold the boat. (Rule 45)

You are vulnerable in the preparatory period because no one is sailing any particular course so the risk of collision is great. However, if you break a rule of Part 2 (the 'when boats meet' rules) you can take a penalty (by getting well clear of other boats and 'doing a 720' as soon as possible after the incident). So unless the infringement is shortly before the starting signal, the penalty is a light one. (Rule 44.1)

If you hit a starting mark, you may exonerate yourself by getting well clear of other boats as soon as possible and 'doing a 360'. (Rule 31.2)

If you are going to sail in championships or open regattas, you need to know the starting penalty signals and systems because they may affect the way you plan your start (balancing the risk of being a premature starter and the reward of getting a cracking good start):

No penalty

The vast majority of races are started with no penalty system in force. The P flag is used as the preparatory signal. You are allowed to be on the course side of the starting line right up to the starting signal. If any part of your boat, crew or equipment is on the wrong side of the line at the moment of the starting signal, you simply have to get back completely behind the line to start properly (known as a 'dip start'). On a starting line with plenty of room, the cost of making a mistake (by crossing prematurely) is small.

The I flag ('Round the ends') penalty system

When an I flag is displayed as the preparatory signal, the 'round the ends' rule will come into effect at the 'one minute signal' (one minute before the starting signal). This means that in the final minute, if any part of your boat is on the course side of the line, you must return to the pre-start side round one of the ends of the line. The idea of the rule is that it stops boats milling around on the course side of the line in the final minute, and encourages boats not to cross the start line prematurely, especially in the middle of the starting line. (Rule 30.1)

The Z flag (20%) penalty system

When a Z flag is displayed as the preparatory signal, if any part of your boat is on the wrong side of the line in the final minute, your finishing position will have 20% of the number of boats entered for the race added on. If any part of your boat is on the wrong side of the line at the start, you must return to start.

The black flag (disqualification)

When a black flag is displayed with the preparatory signal, and in the final minute any part of your boat is on the wrong side of the line, you will be disqualified, unless the race is postponed or abandoned before the starting signal. If there is a general recall you must not start in the next attempt to get the race under way. Even if the race doesn't get started that day, you won't be eligible to start in it when it does get started.

These 'starting penalty' systems can be brought into force for any start. The race committee simply displays the appropriate flag as the preparatory signal.

Now to the boat-to-boat situations......

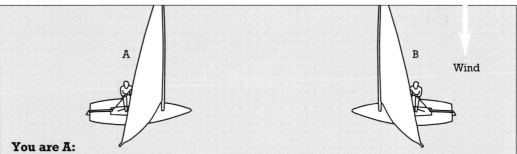

You are A:
• You're on port tack (because your sail is on the starboard side) so you're the give-way boat and you must keep clear. (Rule 10)
• If you change course so that you are no longer on a collision course, and B changes course back onto a collision course, you must change course again and make every effort to keep clear. (Rule 10)

You are B:
• You're the right-of-way boat.
• You may change course, but if you do you must give A room to keep clear, so you mustn't change course so close to A as to prevent him from keeping clear. At a protest hearing, if there is a collision and doubt whether in altering course close to A you failed to give him room, a protest committee is likely to find against you. (Rule 16)

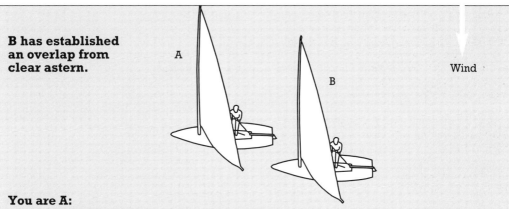

B has established an overlap from clear astern.

You are A:
• While there's no overlap, you may change course as you please; you have no obligations.
• When B gets his overlap to leeward, the situation changes and you must now keep clear of him.
• You need do nothing till there's an overlap, even if you are sitting 'hove-to'; but once he's established the overlap you must manoeuvre to keep clear (by luffing or drawing ahead or even tacking if need be). Bear in mind once he's given you a chance to keep clear, he's allowed to luff right up to head-to-wind. (Rules 11 & 15)

You are B:
• While you are clear astern you must keep clear. (Rule 12)
• You mustn't establish an overlap so close to A that if A luffed or bore away he would immediately make contact (Rules 11, Definition of 'keep clear')
• Once the boats are overlapped, you become the right-of-way boat and may luff right up to head-to-wind. However, you must give A room to keep clear. Even if you don't luff, you can't come charging in while A is hove-to and not initially give him room to pull his sail in and get going. (Rules 11, 15, 16)

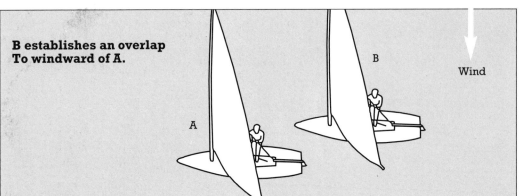

**B establishes an overlap
To windward of A.**

You are A:

• Before the overlap you have no obligations, except that any change of course must be such that it gives B room to keep clear. (Rules 12 & 16)

• When B gets an overlap nothing changes; you may still change course if you wish and you must give B room to keep clear. (Rules 11 & 16)

• You may continue to luff, up to head-to-wind, provided you give B room to keep clear. (Rules 11 & 16)

• However, if there is an obstruction (such as the committee boat) to windward of B which prevents B from responding, then you may not luff; indeed you may even have to bear away to give B room to pass the obstruction. (Rules 18.1, 18.2(a))

You are B:

• You must keep clear before and after you are overlapped. (Rules 12 & 11)

The general principle about windward and leeward situations in the preparatory period is that a leeward boat may luff up to head-to-wind provided she gives the windward boat room to keep clear. It doesn't matter how the overlap was established, or the relative positions fore-and-aft of the two boats. The windward boat must keep clear.

A and B are overlapped approaching an obstruction, (which may or may not be a mark) before they are approaching the line to start.

You are A: You must keep clear, but if B decides to go under the committee boat, you have the right to room if you want to do the same.

You are B: You may choose to go either to windward or to leeward of the committee boat, in spite of any protestations from A. But if you decide to go to windward, you must change course in such a way that A is able to keep clear. If you go to leeward you must give A room to pass under the committee boat if he wants to. (Rules 11, 16 & 18.2(a))

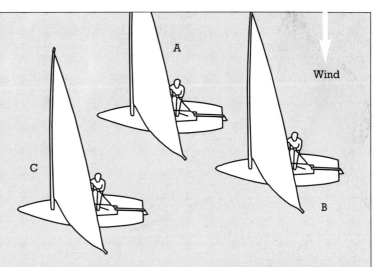

B first gets an overlap to leeward of A, then an overlap to windward of C.

You are A: When B first gets an overlap to leeward of you, because there is a possibility of his bow running into your boom, you must begin to manoeuvre to keep clear. If B luffs after he gets the overlap, you will have to luff too. If B is sailing higher than you are, you'll have to luff, but you don't have to begin to do anything until there is an overlap. (Rule 11)

You are B: When you're astern, you must keep clear. When you first get the overlap to leeward of A, it must not be so close that if A luffs there will immediately be contact. You must give A room to keep clear. Provided you give room, you may luff. You must keep clear of C even if he luffs. If there is not enough room between A and C for you to get between them when you first get your overlap to windward of C, then you don't have the right to go in there. C has the right to luff, and if he chooses to luff the gap will get smaller, so you'll be in a pretty precarious position! (Rules 12, 11, 18.5 & Definition of 'Keep Clear')

You are C: You may luff if you wish, but if you do you must allow B and A room to keep clear. (Rule 16)

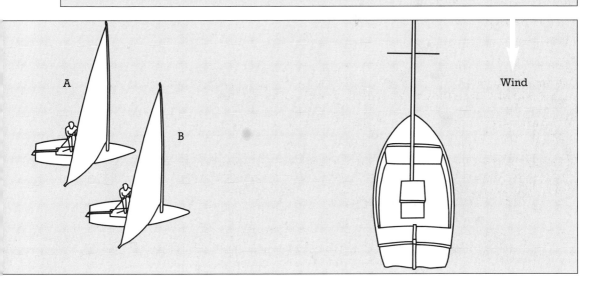

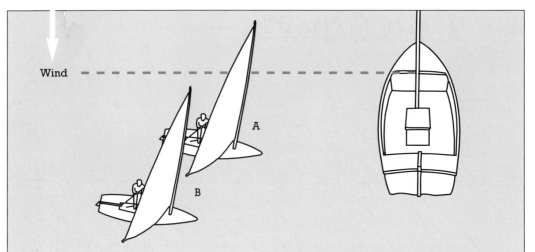

You are A: You have the right to room to pass under the committee boat even though it's a starting mark because you are not 'approaching the line to start'. You don't have to hail, but it's probably a good idea if you think you're not being given enough room. You can change your mind and tack if you want to.

You are B: It is too late now to decide to go to windward of the committee boat, so you must give room to A whether he asks for it or not. You need to give sufficient room for A to pass 'in a seamanlike way'. (Rule 18.2(a))

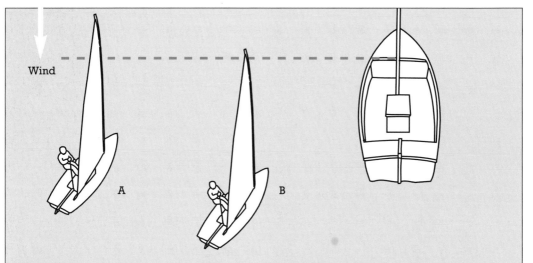

You are A: You are the give-way boat and if B luffs you must keep clear, but if B tacks you become the right-of-way boat while he's tacking and B must keep clear of you. (Rules 11 & 13)

You are B: You have no right to hail for room to tack (whether or not you are approaching the starting line to start) because the committee boat is a starting mark and the rules don't give you the right to room to tack at a starting mark if it's surrounded by navigable water. You had better bear away before you get trapped. If there are any boats to leeward of you they must give you room to pass under the committee boat. (Rule 19.2 & 18.2(a))

4 The Start

This section covers the period from your approach to the starting line shortly before the starting signal, to when you have started and cleared the starting line.

The race committee must make the time between the preparatory signal and the starting signal exactly correct, and must make the correct visual signals at those times. It is allowed to fail to make the sound signal, but the visual signals must be on time. That is why it is important that you check the preparatory signal by watching the committee boat signals (or better still, listening to the time-keeper counting down to the preparatory signal, if you can get close enough); then you can rely on the starting signal being exactly four minutes later. (Rule 26)

When the race committee makes an 'individual recall' signal (when there are premature starters), it must make not only the visual signal (flag X) but also the sound signal (an additional bang or horn). If it doesn't, and you are in doubt as to whether or not you are a premature starter, you may assume you have started correctly and sail on. If the race committee scores you as 'OCS' (On the Course Side at the start) you will be entitled to redress. If you are in no doubt that you are a premature starter, you must return to start properly, whether or not the race committee makes the correct signal. (Rule 29.1, ISAF Case 31)

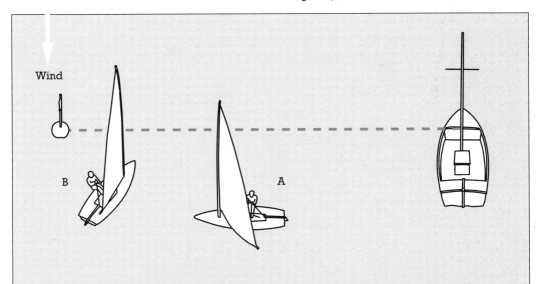

At the moment of the starting signal

You are A: You may want to luff to close-hauled but you may not. B is keeping clear and to luff now would deprive him of room to keep clear. (Rule 16.1)

You are B: You are the give-way boat, but your course and speed will mean you will pass safely ahead of A who is not allowed to change course if that deprives you of room to keep clear. Mind you, if there is an incident and he didn't luff, you'll be likely to lose the protest!

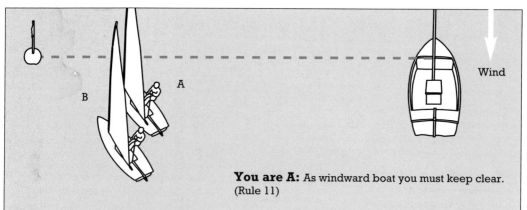

You are A: As windward boat you must keep clear. (Rule 11)

You are B: However you came to be overlapped, (you might have come from astern, or you might have tacked to leeward of A) you may luff (above close-hauled if necessary) to get round the mark, but you must give A room to keep clear. If you established the overlap from clear astern, then you mustn't sail above your proper course, so once you have passed the mark you must bear away to close-hauled or below.

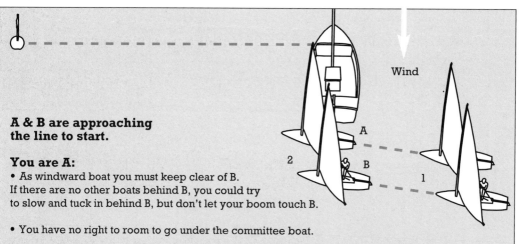

A & B are approaching the line to start.

You are A:
• As windward boat you must keep clear of B.
If there are no other boats behind B, you could try to slow and tuck in behind B, but don't let your boom touch B.

• You have no right to room to go under the committee boat.

• Next time you want to start at the starboard end, don't get caught in this position!

You are B:
• Position 1: Before the starting signal, however the overlap was established, you may luff as high as you like, but if you change course you must give A room to keep clear. If you luff slowly now, A has got room to keep clear by sailing the wrong side of the committee boat. (Rules 11, 16 & 18.1(a))

• After the starting signal, if you established the overlap from clear astern, you must not luff higher than your 'proper course' (close-hauled or the course which takes you just astern of the committee boat). (Rule 17.1)

• If you sail a straight course which allows A enough room to sail astern of the committee boat, then to luff when he cannot escape would not be giving him room. So if you want to shut him out, you need to luff at position 1. (Rules 11, 16 & 18.1(a))

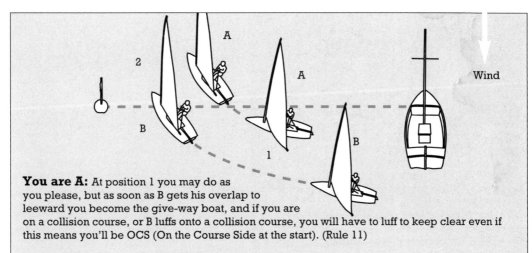

You are A: At position 1 you may do as
you please, but as soon as B gets his overlap to
leeward you become the give-way boat, and if you are
on a collision course, or B luffs onto a collision course, you will have to luff to keep clear even if
this means you'll be OCS (On the Course Side at the start). (Rule 11)

You are B:

• At position 1 you are the give-way boat and must keep clear. (Rule 12)

• When you first get the overlap you become the right-of-way boat, but you must not be so close
to A that he can't keep clear. (Rule 15)

• Before the starting signal you may luff up to head-to-wind but you must give A room to keep
clear (Rule 16)

• At the moment of the starting signal you must promptly bear away to a course no higher than
close-hauled. (Rule 17.1)

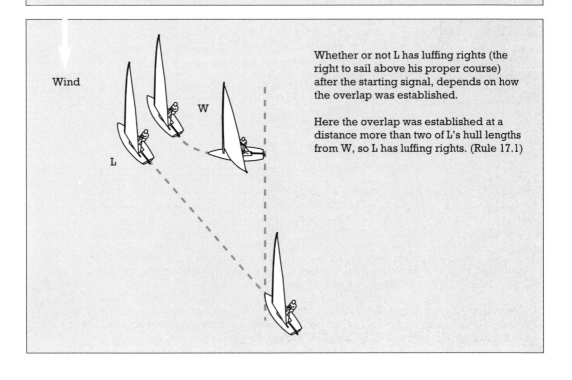

Whether or not L has luffing rights (the
right to sail above his proper course)
after the starting signal, depends on how
the overlap was established.

Here the overlap was established at a
distance more than two of L's hull lengths
from W, so L has luffing rights. (Rule 17.1)

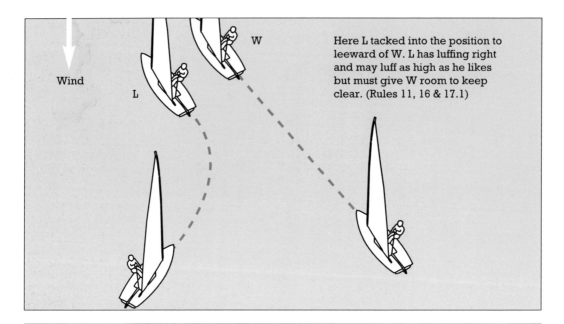

Here L tacked into the position to leeward of W. L has luffing right and may luff as high as he likes but must give W room to keep clear. (Rules 11, 16 & 17.1)

The diagram opposite shows a reaching start. Before the starting signal (when there is no proper course), all the leeward boats (B, D, F and H) may luff up to head-to-wind, if they can give room to the windward boats to keep clear. At the moment of the starting signal, a boat without luffing rights sailing higher than her proper course must bear away. Assuming that their proper courses are to the right of the picture, which of the leeward boats may luff (sail above their proper course) after the starting signal?

You are A or C or E or G: You must keep clear of the leeward boats under you; and you must keep clear of X coming down the start line on starboard tack, and you must not sail below your proper course after the starting signal. (Rules 11, 10, and 17.2)

You are B: You established your overlap from clear astern, but you were more than two lengths away from A at the time. You have luffing rights. You may sail higher than your proper course before or after the start - right up to head-to-wind if A can keep clear. But you must not luff A into the path of X, coming down the start line on starboard tack; in fact you might have to bear away and give more room to A. (Rules 11, 17.1 and 18.2(a))

You are D: You established your overlap from clear astern, and you were within two lengths of C at the time. You are the only leeward boat not to have luffing rights. Before the starting signal (when there is no proper course) you may sail as high as you like, but at the starting signal you must bear away if necessary and then mustn't sail higher than your proper course during the existence of the overlap (unless the gap between the two boats gets to be more than two lengths). (Rules 11 & 17.1)

You are F: E established the overlap to windward of you, so you have luffing rights. You may sail higher than your proper course after the start - right up to head-to-wind if E can keep clear. (Rule 11)

You are H: You established your overlap by completing a tack to leeward of G. You have luffing rights. You may sail higher than your proper course after the start - right up to head-to-wind if G can keep clear. (Rule 11)

You are X: You are not going to be very popular, but as you are on starboard tack you have right-of-way over all the other boats. 'Proper Course' is not relevant when boats are on opposite tacks. (Rule 10)

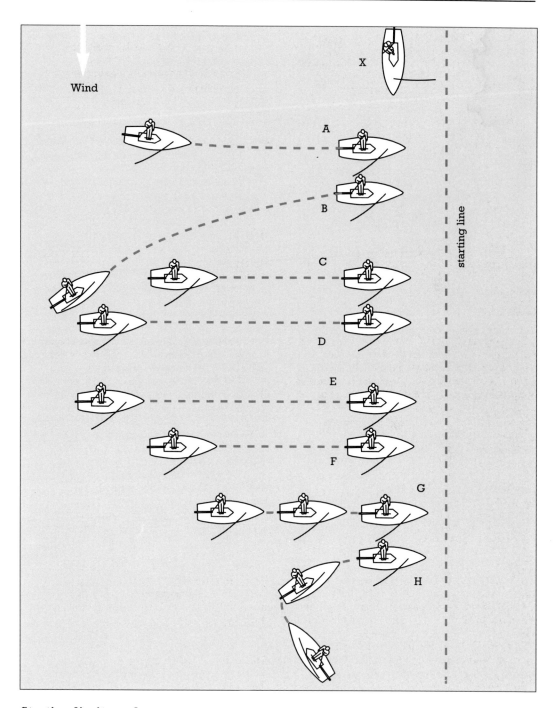

Starting limit marks

Most on-the-water starting lines are between a small buoy (the outer distance mark, or 'ODM') at the port end, and the mast of a committee boat at the starboard end. These must be described in the sailing instructions. Both the ODM and the committee boat are 'marks' because they have a 'required side' when boats start. The committee boat is also an obstruction, and an inside boat therefore has the right to room when everyone is milling about before the start, but not when boats are approaching the line to start. Then no one has the right to room at any starting mark (unless it's not 'surrounded by navigable water').

The most common starting limit mark is the 'inner limit mark' or 'inner distance mark' ('IDM'). Not just the description of the IDM but also the obligations of boats with respect to it must be written into the sailing instructions. You can ignore a sailing instruction like 'There will be an IDM, which will be a yellow mark with a pink flag laid near to the committee boat'.

IDMs cause a lot of problems. The usual reasons one is used are to help protect the committee boat, and to prevent sails very close to the committee boat blocking the race committee's view of the starting line.

Let's look at three examples of a limit mark sailing instruction:

1 'A yellow mark with a pink flag will be laid near the committee boat. Boats shall not pass between this mark and the committee boat after the preparatory signal.'
Strictly speaking, such a sailing instruction does not give the mark a required side (rather it specifies a prohibited area which by definition is an obstruction) so it could be argued that you have the right to room to avoid the 'obstruction', and you may hit the buoy without penalty (provided you don't cross the imaginary line between it and any part of the committee boat); and if you are forced into the 'prohibited area' you can escape penalty by protesting the boat that forced you to break the sailing instruction. (Rule 60.1(a) gives you the right to a hearing and 64.1(b) exonerates you).

2 The most sensible sailing instruction would be: 'A yellow mark with a pink flag will be laid near the committee boat. Boats approaching the line to start shall pass between this mark and the ODM' or 'boats shall pass this mark to starboard'. This would require you to pass the IDM on your starboard side when you are 'approaching the line to start from the pre-course side of the starting line'. Under this sailing instruction, the IDM is a mark because it has a required side, so there is no question of any right to room when you're approaching the line to start. If you get forced the wrong side by someone to leeward who has not broken a rule (for example by their sailing above close-hauled after the starting signal), then you'll just have to sail back and unwind, and pass it on the correct side.

3 In an attempt to really discourage boats from the area between the IDM and the committee boat, the race committee might write a sailing instruction like this: 'A yellow mark with a pink flag will be placed near the committee boat. When approaching the line to start, boats shall pass between this mark and the ODM and after the preparatory signal boats shall not pass between this mark and the committee

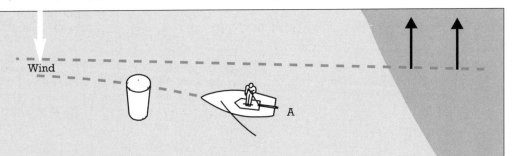

The starting line is formed by extending the transit of the line between the two posts on shore. The ODM has been placed to limit the length of the line.

You are A: When the ODM has drifted behind the line and the port end is favoured, you can gain an advantage. Having passed the ODM on your port side, you'll need to keep sailing towards the line ('approaching the line to start') until you start.

boat'. With this sailing instruction the IDM has a required side, so it is a mark. This means there's no right to room when approaching the line to start and if you get forced between the mark and the committee boat by a boat that didn't break a rule, then you'll have to retire. (I don't recommend such a draconian sailing instruction, but I often see them.)

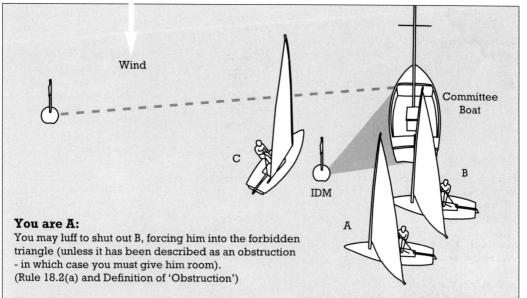

You are A:

You may luff to shut out B, forcing him into the forbidden triangle (unless it has been described as an obstruction - in which case you must give him room).
(Rule 18.2(a) and Definition of 'Obstruction')

You are B:

• You must keep clear of A and you cannot claim room if the IDM has a required side in the sailing instructions. However, if the area between the mark and the committee boat is simply a prohibited area, then A must give you room (whether you ask for it or not, but it's best to hail).
(Rules 18.1(a) & 18.2(a) and Definition of 'Obstruction')

• If you hit the mark but pass it on the correct (starboard) side, you can exonerate yourself by sailing clear and doing a 360 if your only infringement was hitting the mark, or a 720 if you broke a 'when boats meet' rule (for example by not keeping clear of A). If you broke a 'when boats meet' rule *and* you hit the mark, a 720 will exonerate you for both.

• If you are forced the wrong side of the mark, then whether or not you can successfully protest A, or exonerate yourself, all depends on the wording of the sailing instruction.

You are C: If this is the best end to start and the IDM is behind the line you can gain something here by starting right at the end of the line. But having passed the IDM on your starboard side, you must keep sailing towards the line (or you're no longer 'approaching the line to start') and if the sailing instruction prohibits you from sailing between the IDM and the committee boat, you'll need to keep out of the prohibited triangle.

5 The Gate Start

Gate starts are becoming more common in some parts of the world as a way of starting more than eighty or so boats, in a fairly steady wind of Force 3 or more, when there is sufficient room on the water. Discussion will never cease as to whether the gate start or the line start is the fairer, but there is no doubt that to get a good start skippers need different skills and experience. Gate starts can be exciting, and fun.

This is how a gate start works. A pathfinder is appointed. Usually it is one of the competing boats

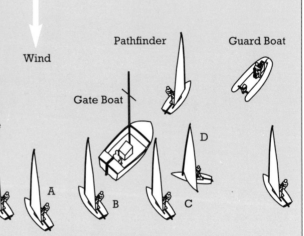

near the top of the fleet. Just before the starting signal he sets off on a port tack close-hauled course. A guard boat is sometimes used, to motor along on the pathfinder's starboard bow, to ensure other boats don't run into the pathfinder and ruin the proceedings.

A gate boat takes up a position astern of the pathfinder, exactly matching the pathfinder's speed and course. Boats then start on starboard tack behind the gate boat. Those that think they sail faster than the pathfinder, or think the left side of the beat is best, start early (near the beginning of the run). Those that think the pathfinder sails faster than they do, or think the right side of the beat is best wait around where they expect the entourage to be, five minutes or so after the starting signal. Knowing the exact time is unimportant; the skill is in 'coming out of the gate' close-hauled at full speed by luffing from a reach to close-hauled, missing the starboard quarter of the gate-boat by a few millimetres. The pathfinder is usually released after five minutes; he can tack any time after being released, gaining a few boat lengths by not having to sail behind the gate boat - a reward for being forced to start at the extreme right side of the beat, and not being allowed to tack on any shifts for the first five minutes.

You are A or B:
• This is really just the same situation as the starboard end of a fixed starting line. You have to keep clear of a boat to leeward, and you have right-of-way over a boat to windward. You must also keep clear of the gate boat.

You are C:
• If you can sail close-hauled without changing course, then you can ignore D. Or you can luff D to force him to luff alongside the gate boat, but you can't luff him into the gate boat, because if you luff you must give him room to keep clear. (Rule 16)

You are D:
• You will need to slow, not to go behind C as you would if this were a fixed-line start, but to be level with him, as are A and B. Remember, the gate-boat is moving at the speed of the pathfinder. You must keep clear of the gate boat. If you touch the gate boat (or the guard boat or - heaven forbid - the pathfinder), you must retire (no chance of a 720) unless you think it wasn't your fault. For example if C forces you to collide with the gate boat by luffing you can hail 'protest', sail on, and lodge a protest after the race.

6 On the Beat

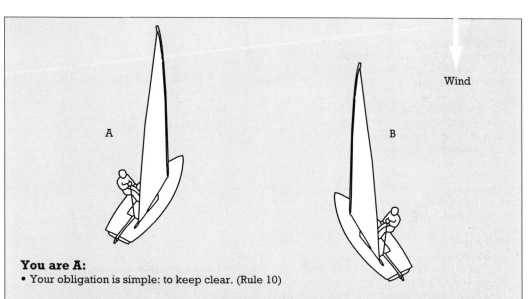

Wind

A

B

You are A:
• Your obligation is simple: to keep clear. (Rule 10)

• If you are going to bear away behind B, you must do it in such a way that B is left in no doubt that you are going to succeed. (Rule 10)

If you decide to tack, you must complete the tack ahead or to leeward of B without B having to change course until your tack is complete. If there is any doubt about whether you tacked far enough from B, a protest hearing is likely to go against you. (Rules 13 & 15)

You are B:
• If you change course you must give room to A to keep clear. Furthermore, if A is keeping clear you mustn't change course if as a result A would immediately need to change course to continue keeping clear. (Rule 16)

• You are not required to hail 'starboard' or anything else, but it is sometimes a good idea to do so if you think that A hasn't seen you because:

1. You must try to avoid contact, and if there is contact and there is damage, you may be penalised. (Rule 14)

2. Even if there is no chance of damage, getting tangled up with a boat required to keep clear can cost many hull-lengths and no redress can be claimed for places lost (unless you are actually damaged by the give-way boat). (Rules 14, 16 & 62.1(b))

• If you want to continue on starboard tack, and don't want A tacking into a position which forces you (from a tactical point of view) to tack, you may bear away and go behind A. You could shout 'Carry on', or 'Pass ahead of me' but nothing you shout puts any obligation on A which he doesn't already have. Although a firm bear-away and/or a hail will often make A decide to carry on, if A is an experienced and skilled racing sailor and is determined to force you into a tactically disadvantageous position, it is not easy to prevent him.

When A completes his tack he is overlapped to leeward of B.

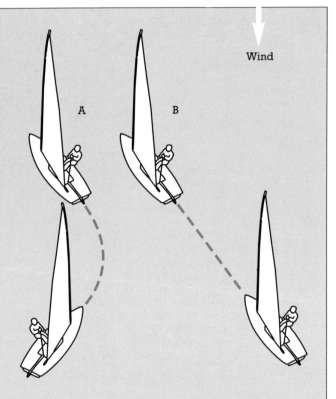

Wind

You are A:

• As you approach on port tack, and while luffing to head-to-wind, your obligation is simple - to keep clear of B. (Rule 10)

• When you pass through head-to-wind and until you are close-hauled on the new tack you must continue to keep clear of B. (Rule 13)

• When your tack is complete, you become the right-of-way boat, but it is only at that instant that B has to begin to take any avoiding action, so you mustn't be in a position where it is impossible or difficult for B to keep clear. Remember that he doesn't have to anticipate that you are going to be there. If he is able to keep clear only by making an unseamanlike manoeuvre, then your tack was too close. (Rule 15)

• When your tack is complete, you have luffing rights, but you cannot use them until you have given B room to keep clear (which requires both space and time). After giving B this opportunity, you may luff above close-hauled if you want to, but your luff must be such that B is able to keep clear. (Rule 16)

You are B:

• You must not change course if by so doing you prevent A from keeping clear, or force him to make an unseamanlike manoeuvre in order to keep clear or force him to change course immediately in response to your change of course. If there is a header (adverse windshift) just as A is tacking, you may be prevented from fulfilling your wish to bear away for a few seconds. You may, of course, tack while A is tacking. (Rule 16)

• You may change course towards A as he approaches on port tack (whether or not there is a windshift), forcing A to tack earlier, provided you give him room to keep clear, and he doesn't have to immediately alter course as a result of you altering your course. (Rule 16)

• Once A's tack is complete and he is to leeward, you become the give-way boat, and you must keep clear even if he luffs. As you will be affected by his back-wind, it's usually tactically sound to tack. (Rule 11)

• Remember that A has luffing rights; once he has given you the opportunity to keep clear he may luff.

• You are not prohibited from tacking, even if A has changed course to keep clear, provided that A has room to keep clear.

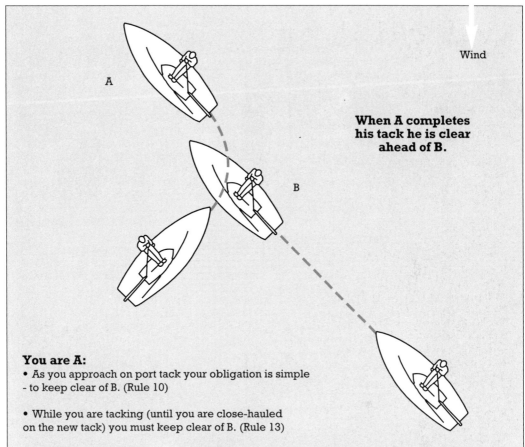

**When A completes
his tack he is clear
ahead of B.**

Wind

You are A:
• As you approach on port tack your obligation is simple
- to keep clear of B. (Rule 10)

• While you are tacking (until you are close-hauled
on the new tack) you must keep clear of B. (Rule 13)

• When your tack is complete you become the right-of-way boat, but it is only at that instant that
B has to begin to take any avoiding action, so you mustn't be in a position where B doesn't have
room to keep clear. Remember that he doesn't have to anticipate that you are going to be there.
If he is able to keep clear only by making an unseamanlike manoeuvre, then your tack was too
close. (Rule 15)

• When you complete your tack you may be sailing more slowly than B, and if B establishes an
overlap to leeward of you, you become the give-way boat again, and you must keep clear.
However, B must not sail above close-hauled unless he promptly sails astern of you (for
example, to tack away). (Rules 11 & 17.1)

You are B:
• You must not change course if by so doing you prevent A from keeping clear, or force him to
make an unseamanlike manoeuvre in order to keep clear, or force him to change course
immediately in response to your change of course. If there is a lift (beneficial windshift) just as A
is passing ahead, you may be prevented from fulfilling your wish to luff for a few seconds. (Rule
16)

• Provided you don't deprive A of room to keep clear, you can tack away at any time. If you get
an overlap to leeward of A, after his tack is complete, you may not sail above close hauled
unless you promptly sail astern of A (for example to tack away). (Rule 17.1)

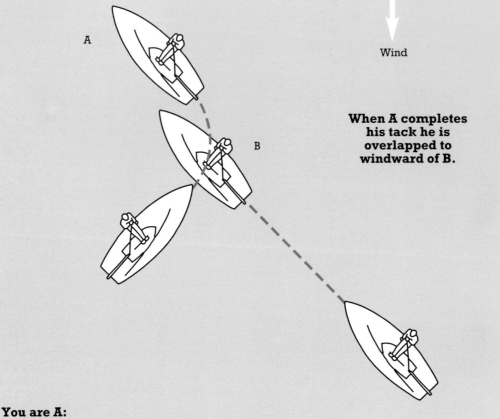

When A completes his tack he is overlapped to windward of B.

You are A:

• As you approach on port tack your obligation is simple - to keep clear of B. (Rule 10)

• While you are tacking (until you are close-hauled on the new tack) you must keep clear of B. (Rule 13)

• When your tack is complete, you are overlapped on B's windward bow putting B in your wind shadow. The manoeuvre is known as a 'slam dunk'. You are still the give-way boat. Furthermore, B has luffing rights and may luff above close-hauled, and you must keep clear. (Rule 11)

You are B:

• You are the right-of-way boat throughout this manoeuvre, and if you do not change course, you do not need to give A room to keep clear. If you change course then you must give A room to keep clear. If there is a lift (beneficial windshift) just as A is passing ahead, you may be prevented from fulfilling your wish to luff for a few seconds. (Rule 16)

• At the completion of A's tack you are overlapped to leeward of A, so you have luffing rights, and may luff above close-hauled, but if you luff you must give A room to keep clear. (Rule 16)

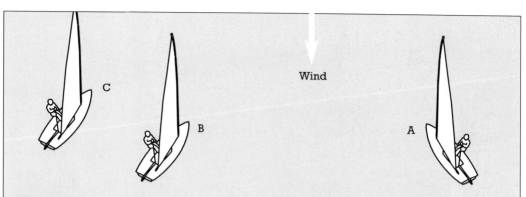

You are A:
- Your rights and obligations are exactly the same as those of boat B on page 29.

You are B:
- You must keep clear of A. (Rule 10)

- You have the right to choose either to go under A's stern or, as you need to change course substantially to avoid A, to tack, irrespective of any hail from C. (Rule 19.1 & Definition of 'Obstruction')

- If you decide to go behind A, you must allow C room to pass under A's stern should he also choose to do so (though unless you are in a team race and C is an opponent, he'd probably rather tack). (Rule 18.2(a))

- If you decide to tack, you must hail C for room to tack (something like 'room to tack' or 'water for a starboard boat') and then tack as soon as you can do so without colliding with C. You need to hail early enough to allow C time to respond to your hail before you have a problem with A. This is especially important if there are boats to windward of C. (Rule 19.1)

- You must not hail C for room to tack, and then go behind A (unless C does not respond to the hail). (Rule 19.1)

- If you decide to hail for room to tack, and C does not respond, hail again more loudly. The pivotal issue in a protest in relation to this situation is often whether or not the hail was made; the helmsman of the leeward boat says he hailed, and the helmsman of the hailed boat says he didn't hear a hail. The protest committee will be more inclined to find as fact that a hail was made if it has been repeated more loudly.

- If you can keep clear of A by making only a small (or no) change of course, then you do not have the right to hail and must pass under A, giving room to C if he chooses to go under A as well. (Rules 18.2(a), 19.1, Definition of Obstruction, ISAF Case 3)

You are C:
- Obviously you may tack if you want to.

- You must keep clear of A, and as windward boat you must keep clear of B if he luffs. If B sails behind A, then provided that in your opinion (you must be reasonable) you cannot safely cross in front of A, you have the right to go behind A, and B must give you room (whether or not you ask for it) provided you had an inside overlap when B was two lengths from A. (Rules 10, 11 & 18)

- If B hails for room to tack, then you must either immediately tack, or hail 'you tack' and take on the responsibility of keeping clear. If you choose to tack, you don't have to carry out the tack any faster than is normal for you, but you must begin the manoeuvre immediately. If there are boats to windward of you preventing you from tacking, you must hail them for room and tack when it is safe to do so. You are under no obligation to tack unless and until B hails for room. (Rule 19.1)

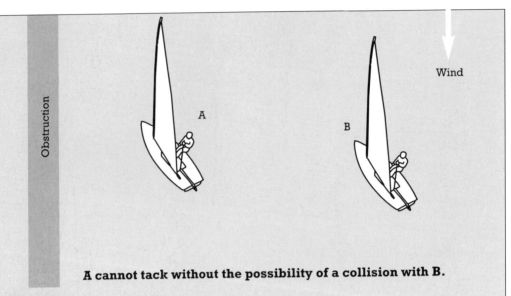

A cannot tack without the possibility of a collision with B.

You are A:
• You will need room to tack, and you know that if you do B will be in the way, so you have the right to hail B for room to tack. (Rule 19.1)

• You are permitted to hail only if you really believe there is an obstruction ahead, but underwater weed or shallows count as an obstruction.

• Until you hail, B is under no obligation to do anything. (Rule 19.1)

• If he doesn't respond to the first hail, hail again more loudly.

• If there is a boat to windward or astern of B that would prevent him from tacking, you will need to hail in time for him to hail for room. (Rule 19.1)

• If he responds by tacking, you must tack as soon as possible even if there is a lift (advantageous windshift) and you'd like to change your mind and continue sailing near the shore out of an adverse tide. (Rule 19.1(a))

• If he responds by hailing 'you tack', you must tack as soon as possible. (Rule 19.1(b))

You are B:
• You must keep clear if A luffs to head-to-wind because you will be windward or astern. (Rules 11 & 12)

• Although you are under no obligation to do anything until A hails, if it's windy and noisy, you should be reasonably attentive to his need to hail.

• In response to his hail you must either tack as soon as possible or immediately hail back 'you tack'.

• If you want to tack but cannot tack because of a boat to windward or astern, you must hail that boat for room to tack and tack as soon as possible. (Rule 19)

• If you hail 'you tack' you must keep clear of A while he tacks, and having completed his tack, you have to give him room to keep clear. (Rule 19.1(b))

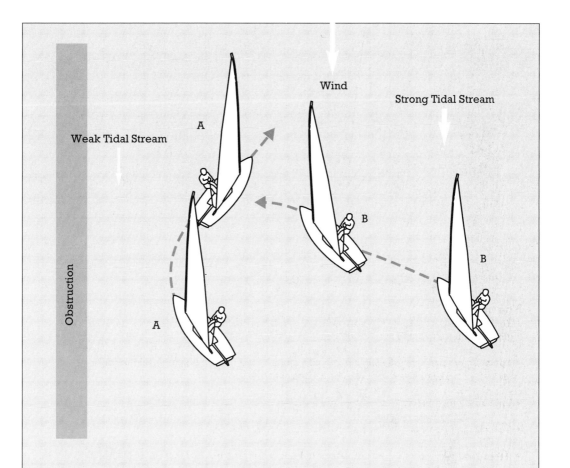

A wants to tack but is unsure whether he can tack and clear B.
So A has the right to hail B for room to tack. A hails 'Room to tack'.
B replies 'You tack'.

You are A:
• Having hailed for room to tack, you must tack immediately there is room, even if there is a lift (advantageous windshift) and you'd like to continue sailing near the shore out of the adverse tidal stream. (Rule 19.1(a))

• When you have completed your tack you become the give-way boat and you must try to keep clear of B. In this diagram there is nothing you can do except sail straight on, so you can sail on and you have broken no rule. (Rules 10 and 19.1(b))

You are B:
When you hail 'You tack' you undertake to keep clear of A while he tacks, and having completed his tack, you must give him room to keep clear. You can give A room by bearing off behind him. If you do so, no rule is broken. (Rule 19.1(b))

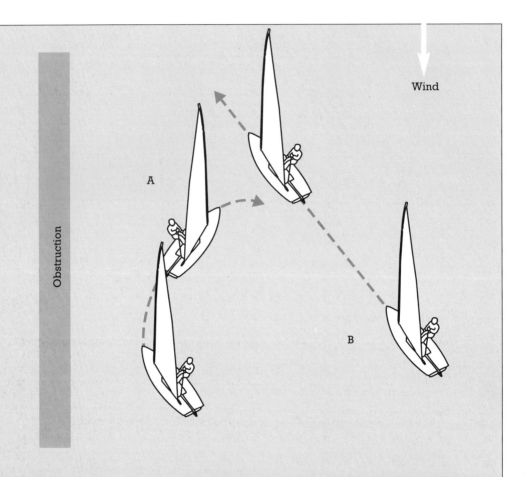

A wants to tack but is unsure whether he can tack and clear B. So A has the right to hail B for room to tack. A hails 'Room to tack'. B replies 'You tack'.

You are A:
• Having hailed for room to tack, you must tack immediately there is room, even if there is a lift (advantageous windshift) and you'd like to continue sailing near the shore out of the adverse tidal stream. (Rule 19.1(a))

• When you have completed your tack you become the give-way boat and you must try to keep clear of B. If you can bear away under B's stern without difficulty (as you can in this diagram), then you must do so. You become required to keep clear only when your tack is complete, and if you then cannot keep clear, or you manage to keep clear but only by making an unseamanlike manoeuvre, then B has broken Rule 19 and you should protest. (Rules 10 & 19.1(b)))

You are B:
When you hail 'You tack' you undertake to keep clear of A while he tacks, but having completed his tack, you have to give him room to keep clear. In this diagram you have done so; A can easily bear off behind you, so no rule is broken. (Rules 10 & 19.1(b))

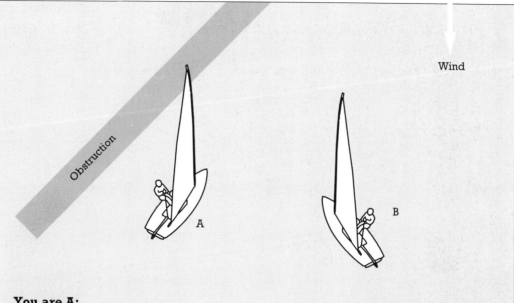

You are A:

• You are in big trouble. You don't have the right to room, and the obstruction prevents you from tacking. If you force B to change course, you must take a 720 penalty. (Rules 10 & 44.1)

• You should have thought of this possibility earlier when there was time to bear away under B!

You are B:

• You could be Mr. Nice Guy and tack now, or you could sail on till you are forced to tack to avoid contact with A, in which case A will have broken Rule 10 and must take a penalty. (Rules 10 & 44.1)

7 Rounding the Windward Mark

Rounding a port-hand windward mark

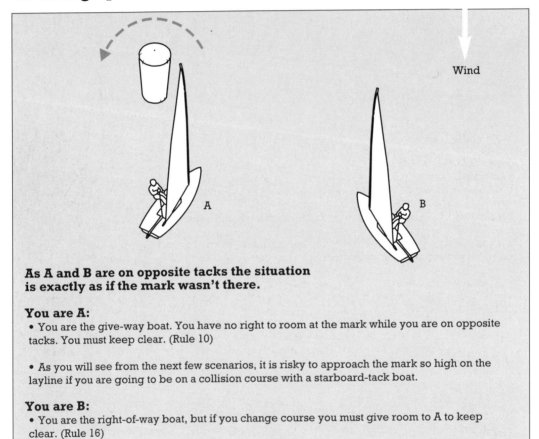

As A and B are on opposite tacks the situation is exactly as if the mark wasn't there.

You are A:
• You are the give-way boat. You have no right to room at the mark while you are on opposite tacks. You must keep clear. (Rule 10)

• As you will see from the next few scenarios, it is risky to approach the mark so high on the layline if you are going to be on a collision course with a starboard-tack boat.

You are B:
• You are the right-of-way boat, but if you change course you must give room to A to keep clear. (Rule 16)

A tacks into a position overlapped to leeward of B, completing his tack when more than two lengths from the mark.

You are A:
• As you approach on port tack, you are the give-way boat and must keep clear. (Rule 10)

• While you are tacking you are the give-way boat and must keep clear. (Rule 13)

• You have completed the tack just outside two boat-lengths, and you are overlapped inside B. You

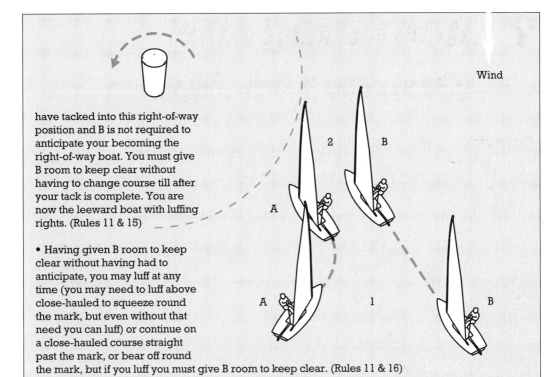

have tacked into this right-of-way position and B is not required to anticipate your becoming the right-of-way boat. You must give B room to keep clear without having to change course till after your tack is complete. You are now the leeward boat with luffing rights. (Rules 11 & 15)

• Having given B room to keep clear without having had to anticipate, you may luff at any time (you may need to luff above close-hauled to squeeze round the mark, but even without that need you can luff) or continue on a close-hauled course straight past the mark, or bear off round the mark, but if you luff you must give B room to keep clear. (Rules 11 & 16)

• If your only proper course is to gybe around the mark you must not sail higher than your proper course as you round the mark. (Rule 18.4)

• If B is not able to keep clear while you luff to pass the mark because there are several other boats to windward of him, then you do not have the right to tack under him and sail your proper course round the mark. (Rule 18.2(d))

• If there is 'reasonable doubt' as to whether either of you were two lengths from the mark when your tack was complete, you must presume that you are too late to get the right to round inside B. (Rule 18.2(e))

You are B:
• While A is approaching on port tack and while he's tacking you mustn't change course to prevent him from keeping clear, or force him to immediately change course if he's keeping clear. This doesn't stop you bearing away early to force him to tack earlier to avoid you, provided he can do it without difficulty. (Rules 13 & 16)

• If you are forced to change course before A has completed his tack, A will have broken Rule 13.

• However, if A completes his tack outside two boat-lengths, he becomes the right of way boat, and you must keep clear. He has luffing rights and unless his only proper course is to gybe around the mark, he may luff at any time as high as he likes, or sail straight on. You must keep clear. (Rules 11 & 18.2(a))

• If A's tack was completed when either of you were within two lengths of the mark, then A has no right to force you to sail above close-hauled. You can protest but you must still keep clear. (Rules 18.2(e), 18.3(a) & 11)

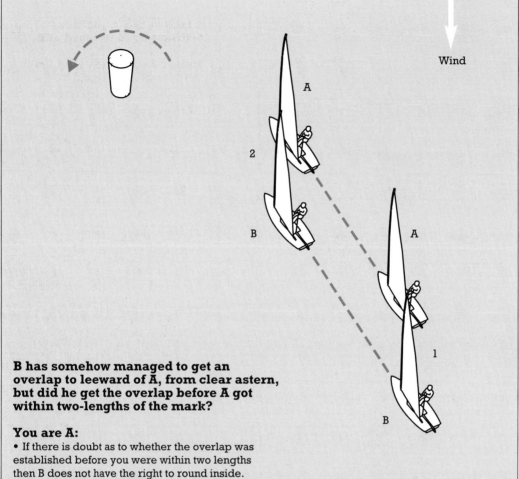

**B has somehow managed to get an
overlap to leeward of A, from clear astern,
but did he get the overlap before A got
within two-lengths of the mark?**

You are A:
• If there is doubt as to whether the overlap was
established before you were within two lengths
then B does not have the right to round inside.
It is a good idea to tell him so, and keep clear. (Rule 18.2(e))

• Because B got his overlap from clear astern, he has no luffing rights, but if the overlap is
established before you were two lengths from the mark, then he may sail his proper course
around the mark, and you must keep clear. His proper course is a wide rounding if that's how
he would round without you being there. You must keep clear. (Rule 18.2(a))

You are B:
• If the boats become overlapped, without doubt, before A comes within two lengths of the mark,
and are overlapped at the two hull-length zone, you have the right to sail your proper course as
you round the mark. This means you may sail the course you would have sailed in the absence of
A, even if this means sailing above close-hauled to 'shoot' the mark. You may even head up a bit
so that you don't get too far from the mark as you complete the rounding. (Rule 18.2(a))

• If there is 'reasonable doubt' as to whether A was two lengths from the mark when you
established the overlap, you must presume that you are too late. If A is shouting to you that
your overlap is too late, you'd be wise to keep clear. (Rule 18.2(e))

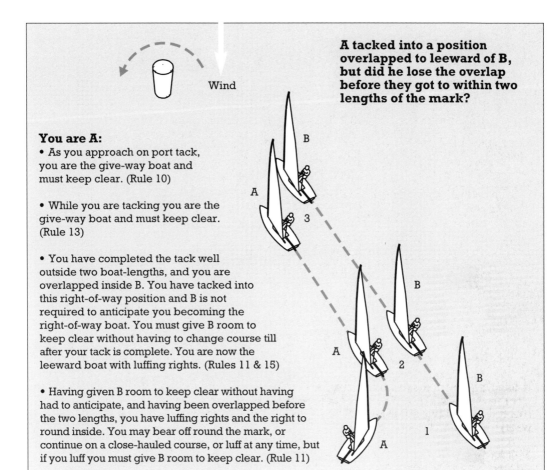

Wind

A tacked into a position overlapped to leeward of B, but did he lose the overlap before they got to within two lengths of the mark?

You are A:
• As you approach on port tack, you are the give-way boat and must keep clear. (Rule 10)

• While you are tacking you are the give-way boat and must keep clear. (Rule 13)

• You have completed the tack well outside two boat-lengths, and you are overlapped inside B. You have tacked into this right-of-way position and B is not required to anticipate you becoming the right-of-way boat. You must give B room to keep clear without having to change course till after your tack is complete. You are now the leeward boat with luffing rights. (Rules 11 & 15)

• Having given B room to keep clear without having had to anticipate, and having been overlapped before the two lengths, you have luffing rights and the right to round inside. You may bear off round the mark, or continue on a close-hauled course, or luff at any time, but if you luff you must give B room to keep clear. (Rule 11)

• Only if your only proper course is to gybe around the mark must you not sail higher than your proper course as you round the mark. (Rule 18.4)

• If there is 'reasonable doubt' as to whether either of you were two lengths from the mark when your tack was complete, you must not force B to sail above close-hauled. (Rules 18.2(e), 18.3(a))

You are B:
• While A is approaching on port tack and while he's tacking you mustn't change course to prevent him from keeping clear or make it difficult for him to keep clear, or force him to immediately alter course. This doesn't stop you bearing away early to force him to tack earlier to avoid you, provided he can keep clear without difficulty. (Rules 13 & 16)

• If you are forced to change course before A has completed his tack, A will have broken Rule 13.

• As A completes his tack outside two boat-lengths, he becomes the right of way boat, and you must keep clear. He has luffing rights and unless his only proper course is to gybe around the mark, he may luff at any time or sail straight on. You must keep clear. (Rules 11 & 18.2(a))

• If there is doubt as to whether you have broken the overlap when you come within two lengths of the mark, then A has the right to room. If A is shouting to you that he is overlapped at two lengths, you'd be wise to keep clear. (Rule 18.2(e))

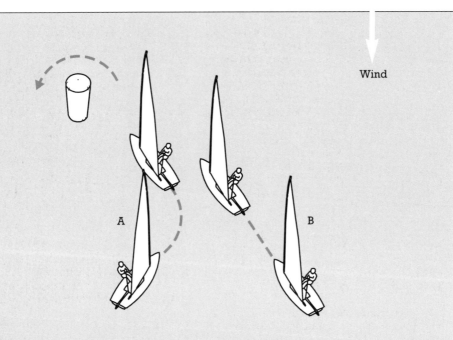

Wind

A

B

A completes his tack onto starboard within two lengths of the mark, ahead or to leeward of B.

You are A:
• As you approach on port tack, you are the give-way boat and must keep clear. (Rule 10)

• While you are tacking you are the give-way boat and must keep clear. (Rule 13)

• You have completed the tack within two hull-lengths of the mark. You have tacked into this right-of-way position but B is not required to anticipate your having become the right-of-way boat. You must give B room to keep clear without having to change course till after your tack is complete. (Rule 15)

• Now you have another problem. Even after your tack is complete, you must not force B (who is probably sailing faster than you are) to luff above close-hauled in order to avoid you. (Rule 18.3(a))

You are B:
• While A is approaching on port tack and while he's tacking you mustn't change course to prevent him from keeping clear or make it difficult for him to keep clear. This doesn't stop you bearing away early to force him to tack earlier to avoid you, provided he can keep clear without difficulty. (Rules 13 & 16)

• If you are forced to change course before A has completed his tack, A will have broken Rule 13.

• If A completes his tack to leeward of you he becomes the right of way boat, but if you can avoid him only by sailing above close-hauled (which is almost inevitable in this diagram) then he has broken Rule 18.3(a) and must take a penalty.

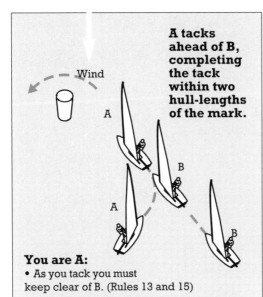

A tacks ahead of B, completing the tack within two hull-lengths of the mark.

Wind

You are A:

• As you tack you must keep clear of B. (Rules 13 and 15)

• If you complete your tack without forcing B to change course to avoid you, the next thing you have to worry about is that if B, with superior speed, can avoid you only by sailing above his close-hauled course, then you have broken a rule, and must take a penalty. (Rules 15 & 18.3(a))

• Furthermore, if B chooses to bear away and gets an overlap to leeward of you, you must keep clear while B rounds the mark. (Rule 18.3(b))

• Whatever you do you mustn't prevent B from passing the mark. (Rule 18.3(a))

• Basically, for this manoeuvre to succeed, you must stay clear ahead until B has rounded or passed the mark (that is, until B has left the mark astern).

You are B:

• When A's tack is complete, you become the give-way boat, but if the only way you can avoid him is to luff above your close-hauled course, he has broken a rule and must take a penalty. (Rule 18.3(a))

• If you choose to bear away and get an overlap to leeward of A, A must keep clear while you round or pass the mark. You mustn't sail higher than your proper course. Rules 17.1 & 18.3(b))

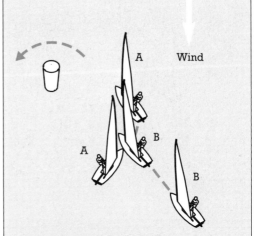

Wind

A completes his tack within two lengths of the mark nearly overlapped, or overlapped to windward of B.

You are A:

• As you tack you must keep clear of B. (Rules 13 and 15)

• If at the moment you pass through head-to-wind B is overlapped to leeward, then B has luffing rights. You must continue to keep clear of B even if B luffs right up to head-to-wind. (Rule 11)

• If at the moment your tack is complete B is clear astern, and chooses to go between you and the mark, you must give room to B who is allowed to sail his proper course (the course he would have sailed had you not been there). (Rule 18.3(b))

You are B:

• If you were clear astern when A completed his tack, you may choose to go inside if you want to, and then sail your proper course (the course you would have sailed had A not been there). (Rule 18.3(b))

• If you were overlapped to leeward of A when A completed his tack, you have luffing rights and you may sail any course, but if you luff you must give A room to keep clear. However, if your only proper course is to gybe at the mark, you can sail your proper course but no higher. (Rules 11, 16 & 18.4)

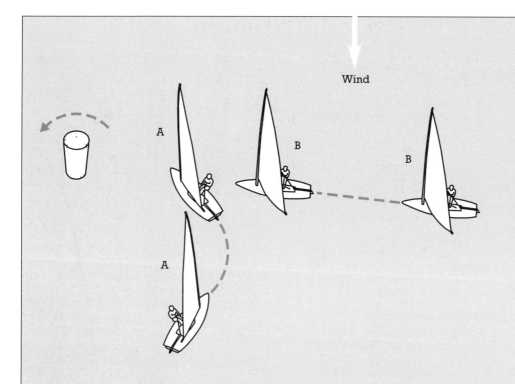

A tacks within two lengths of the mark to leeward or ahead of B who is approaching on a reach (perhaps having overstood the mark).

You are A:
• You must complete your tack without forcing B to change course to keep clear. (Rule 13)

• After you have completed your tack, you mustn't force B to sail above his close-hauled course in order to keep clear of you. (Rule 18.3(a))

• Even though you have luffing rights, you must not prevent B from passing the mark. (Rule 18.3(a))

• Once B has passed the mark (left it astern) you may luff (you have luffing rights) but if you do you must give B room to keep clear. (Rules 11 & 16)

You are B:
• You need do nothing till A's tack is complete, then you must keep clear, but if the only way you can keep clear is by sailing above close-hauled, then A must take a 720 degree penalty. (Rule 18.3(a))

Rounding a starboard-hand windward mark

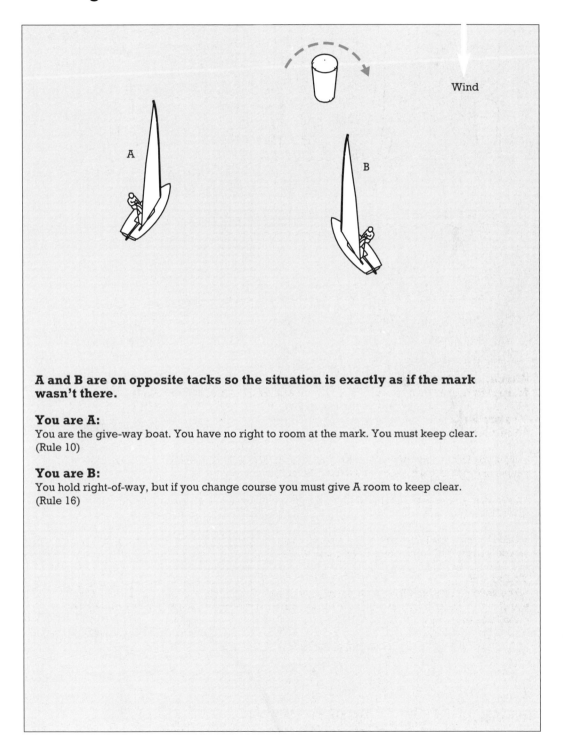

A and B are on opposite tacks so the situation is exactly as if the mark wasn't there.

You are A:
You are the give-way boat. You have no right to room at the mark. You must keep clear. (Rule 10)

You are B:
You hold right-of-way, but if you change course you must give A room to keep clear. (Rule 16)

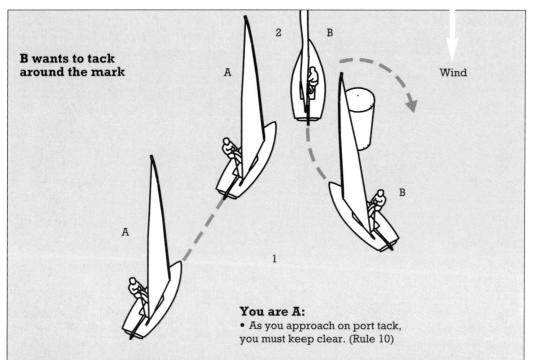

B wants to tack around the mark

Wind

You are A:
• As you approach on port tack, you must keep clear. (Rule 10)

• At position 2, B has luffed to head-to-wind. He is still on starboard tack. You must keep clear. (Rule 10)

• If you keep clear by luffing, you must not end up so close alongside him that any change of course he makes will result in immediately making contact. (Rule 10 and the Definition of 'Keep Clear'.)

• If you luff and tack, you must keep clear. (Rule 13)

You are B:
• As A approaches you must not change course so as to make it difficult for A to keep clear. However, the luff to get to position 2 has fulfilled this obligation, as A can easily keep clear by luffing. (Rule 16)

• At position 2 you must not turn any more, because once you go through head-to-wind you become the give-way boat, and A is so close behind that he will be forced to change course. (Rule 13)

• If A ducks your stern, leaving the mark on the wrong side, you'll probably be able to tack but you will be the give-way boat while you're tacking, and you'll probably be the windward boat when you've completed your tack. In either case you must keep clear. (Rules 13 & 11)

• If A luffs to avoid you when you're head-to-wind, and gets overlapped on your port side, although you remain the right-of-way boat till he goes through head-to-wind, if you bear away you must give him room to keep clear. (Rule 16)

• If A tacks, then immediately he is past head-to-wind you can complete your tack. (Rule 13)

• The best tactic in this scenario if you haven't room to complete a tack before A gets too close, is to slow down at position 1 to force A to tack, then tack.

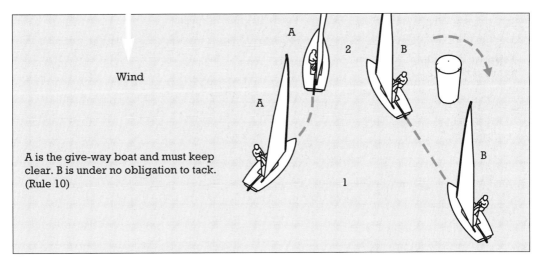

A is the give-way boat and must keep clear. B is under no obligation to tack. (Rule 10)

You are A:
You were keeping clear of B by passing ahead. B has altered course so he must give you room to keep clear. (Rule 16)

You are B:
As much as you may like to luff to tack around the mark, you cannot do this if the change of course doesn't give A room to keep clear. (Rule 16)

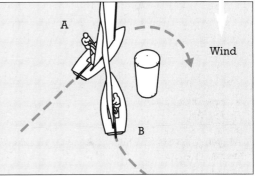

You are A:
- At position 1 when you begin to luff to tack, you are clear ahead and, therefore, the right-of-way boat.

- When you go through head-to-wind you must keep clear of B. Because B has luffed you may be prevented from completing your tack. (Rule 13)

- Next time you approach the mark with an opponent close astern, try to be on the layline, rather than half a length to leeward.

You are B:
- As A luffs to head-to-wind, you may luff too. You don't have to anticipate that he is going to tack.

- When A goes through head-to-wind you become the right-of-way boat, so if you change course after he goes through head-to-wind, you must give him room to keep clear. In the diagram he does have room - he can bear away. (Rules 12, 10 & 16)

- To prevent A from tacking in front of you, you need to luff till he reaches head-to-wind, then sail straight. Tack when there's room.

When the windward mark is an obstruction

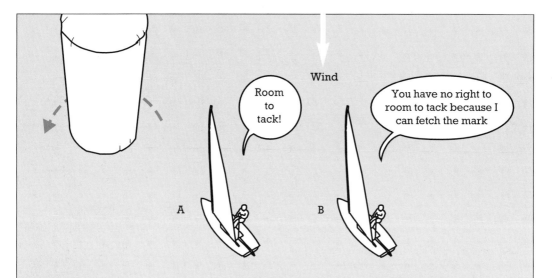

This situation occurs only when the mark is also an obstruction (but not if it's a starting mark when approaching the line to start). The mark might be a large metal buoy or a boat.

You are A:
• Provided that you need to make more than a minor change of course to avoid the obstruction, you may hail to B for room to tack. 'Water' may be misunderstood; 'Room to tack' is best. (Rule 19.1)

• If B chooses not to tack, and then fails to fetch the mark (that is, he goes beyond head-to-wind to get round), then he has broken a rule and you should protest him. (Rule 19.2)

• Even if B can get round the mark without going beyond head-to-wind, you are still the right-of-way boat provided you don't go beyond head-to-wind yourself, so even if you don't have luffing rights, you may go up to head-to-wind in order to 'shoot the mark', and B must keep clear. (Rule 11 & Definition of 'Proper Course')

• For you to have the right to hail, you have to be on a course from which you must make a substantial change to avoid the obstruction. If you were further to leeward, so that the obstruction was not in your path, then you would not have the right to hail; you would have to slow down and tack behind B or bear off and gybe. (Definition of 'obstruction')

You are B:
• As the windward boat you must keep clear if A luffs in an attempt to 'shoot the mark'. (Rule 11)

• If A hails for room to tack, and you are sure that you can get round the mark without tacking, then you may refuse to tack, but if he luffs remember you are the windward boat and must keep clear. (Rule 11)

• If A hails for room to tack, and you are not sure that you can get round the mark without tacking, then you must either tack or hail back 'you tack' and give room to A to tack. (Rule 19)

8 On the Reach

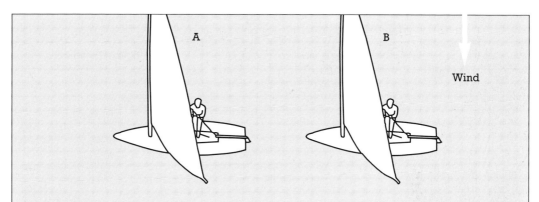

You are A: You are the right-of-way boat and you may change course as you please. (Rule 12)

You are B: Your only obligation is to keep clear of A (because you are 'clear astern'), but you may sail any course you like. (Rule 12)

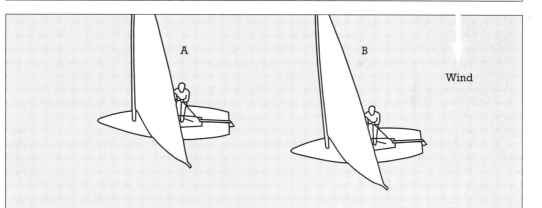

You are A:
• If B is within two hull-lengths of you and heading towards your leeward side, you must not sail below your proper course (see the definition of proper course on pages 12 & 13). (Rule 17.2)

• If there are waves to be played, you can play them. If there are boats to windward or astern likely to take your wind, you can luff or bear away to get clear air. You simply mustn't sail lower than you would have done in the absence of B. (Rules 12 & 17.2)

You are B:
• As you are the boat clear astern, you must keep clear of A, but while there is no overlap you have no other obligations and may change course as you please. (Rule 12)

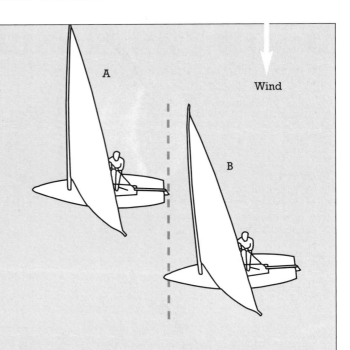

You are A:

• After B gets an overlap, you continue to be required not to sail below your proper course, but you now have a new obligation - to keep clear, even if B sails a course higher than your own. (Rules 17.2 & 11)

• If B sails a course you think is higher than his proper course, you may protest, but you must still keep clear. (Rule 11)

• If B sails very low (in an effort to hold on to clear wind), you continue to be obliged not to sail below your proper course while the gap between you is anything up to two hull-lengths. (Rules 11 & 17.2)

You are B:

• When you get your overlap to leeward of A, you will become the right-of-way boat, but A doesn't have to anticipate your getting the overlap, so you must initially give him room to keep clear. (Rule 15)

• Once you've done this, although you don't have luffing rights, you may sail up to, but not above, your proper course. You must not sail above your proper course while the overlap exists and you are within two hull-lengths of A. (Rules 11 & 17.1)

• If you luff (up to your proper course), you must give A room to keep clear. (Rule 16)

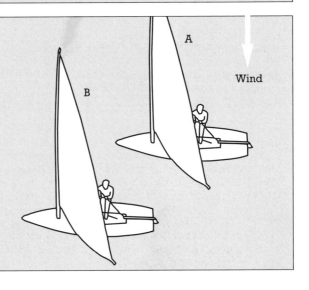

B having established an overlap to leeward of A, has somehow advanced nearly a hull-length through A's lee. There is no change in rights and obligations. B may sail as high as his proper course, and A must keep clear. A might be forced to sail higher than his own proper course, but nevertheless he must keep clear.

The boats are in the same positions as they were in the previous diagram, but here the situation has arisen through A establishing an overlap from astern to windward of B. The boats' rights and obligations are quite different, because B has luffing rights.

You are A:
• You must keep clear of B. (Rule 11)

• You must not sail below your proper course whilst the overlap exits (and the gap between the two boats is less than two lengths). (Rule 17.2)

You are B:
• You may sail any course but if you luff you must give A room to keep clear. (Rule 16)

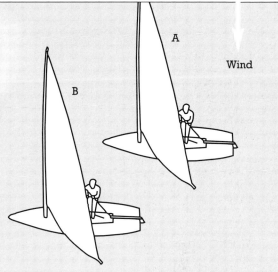

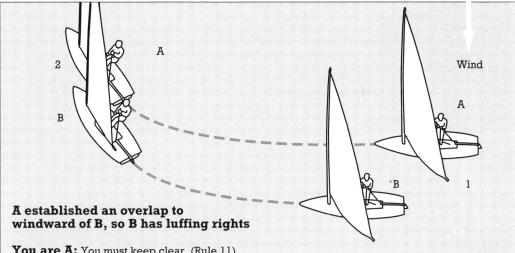

A established an overlap to windward of B, so B has luffing rights

You are A: You must keep clear. (Rule 11)

You are B: You may luff or bear away as you please provided you give A room to keep clear. (Rule 16)

The 'lock-up' position:
• At position 2, if A luffs, his stern will swing into B. If he bears away their courses will converge and there will be contact almost immediately. The only way in which A can fulfil his obligation to keep clear is to sail straight on. B can luff no more, for to do so would not be giving A room to keep clear. B may continue sailing straight ahead, or he may bear away. (Rules 11 & 16).

• It is for this reason that luffing a boat to windward is rarely worthwhile in fleet racing. B would be wise to luff to clear his wind before A gets an overlap to windward and, unless there is a port rounding mark coming up soon, encourage A to overtake to leeward.

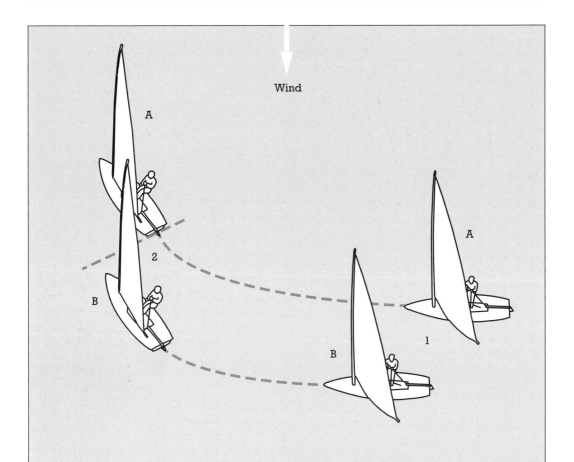

Wind

A

A

2

B

B

1

A establishes an overlap to windward of B. At position 2 the overlap is broken.

You are A:
• Position 1: You established the overlap from clear astern to windward of B, so B has luffing rights. You must keep clear. (Rule 11)

• Position 2: When the overlap is broken, your only obligation is not to sail below your proper course, unless you gybe. (Rule 17.2)

You are B:
• Position 1: You have luffing rights and may luff as high as you please but you must give A room to keep clear. (Rule 16)

• Position 2: When A draws ahead and the overlap is broken, you become clear astern and must therefore keep clear, but you may sail any course. (Rule 12)

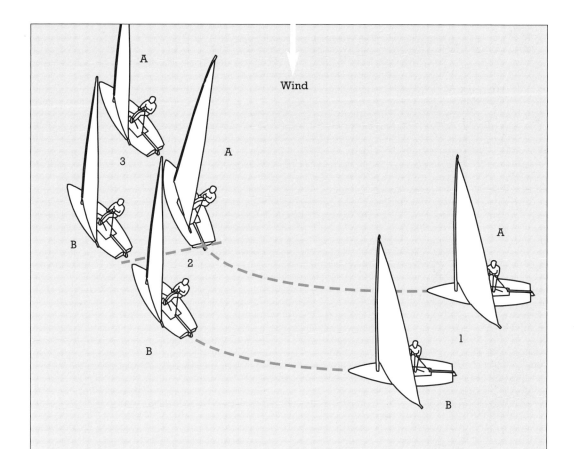

A established the overlap to windward of B.

You are A:
• Position 1: You established the overlap from clear astern to windward of B, so B has luffing rights. You must keep clear. (Rule 11)

• Position 2: You can luff to break the overlap so that B becomes clear astern and must keep clear.

• Position 3: When you bear away and an overlap is re-established, B must bear away to his proper course (or lower). However, you are still the give-way boat and must keep clear. Furthermore, because it was your action that put you into a give-way position, B does not initially have to give you room to keep clear. (Rules 11 & 15)

You are B:
• Position 1: You have luffing rights and may luff as high as you please but you must give A room to keep clear. (Rule 16)

• Positions 2 & 3: When A luffs to break the overlap, and then bears away to re-establish an overlap, you lose your luffing rights. You must immediately bear away to your proper course (or lower). If to sail your proper course you need to gybe, then you must gybe. (Rule 17.1)

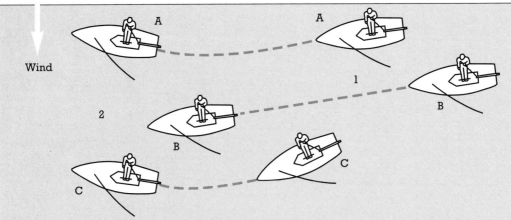

In this scenario, B establishes an overlap from clear astern to leeward of A, then while still overlapped with A, B gets an overlap to windward of C.

You are A:
• You are under no obligation to anticipate B getting an overlap, but when he does you must keep clear. Even if B does not luff, you will have to luff to avoid him running into your boom. (Rules 12 & 11)

You are B:
• When you first get an overlap to leeward of A, you must give him room to keep clear. Then you may sail up to your proper course, but no higher. (Rules 15, 16 & 17.1)

• Your proper course is the course that keeps clear of C. (Definition of 'Proper Course')

• If C luffs, you must keep clear of C who has luffing rights over both you and A, because you both established overlaps on C's windward side. (Rule 11)

You are C:
• You have luffing rights over both A and B so may luff as high as you like, but you must give them room to keep clear. (Rule 16)

Passing obstructions

You are A:
• You are the windward boat so you must keep clear of B. (Rule 11)

• If B sails to leeward of the obstruction, you may also go to leeward only if that is a proper course for you. If you do go to leeward, B must give you room, but as soon as the obstruction has been passed, you must keep clear. (Rules 11, 17.2, 18.2(a))

You are B:
• If you have luffing rights, you may luff A at any time and obviously may go to windward of the obstruction. If you change course you must give A room to keep clear. (Rules 11 & 16)

• If you don't have luffing rights you may only pass to windward of the island if that is a proper course for you. Both sides are sometimes proper courses. (Rule 17.1)

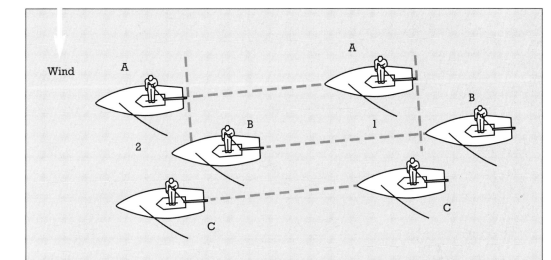

B is already overlapped with C when he gets an overlap to leeward of A.

You are B: C (the right-of-way boat) counts as a 'continuing obstruction'. When you first get the overlap between A and the continuing obstruction, was there sufficient room for you to pass between them? If you freeze the picture at position 2, and the answer is 'no', you have no right to room. You should have sailed to leeward of C or to windward of A. (Rule 18.5)

• Whether or not you have luffing rights, if you choose to go to leeward, and A chooses to do likewise, you must give him room to pass between you and the obstruction. (Rule 18.2(a))

• If you both sail to leeward of the obstruction, once the island has been passed, if you have luffing rights you may luff above your proper course, but you must give A room to keep clear. (Rule 16)

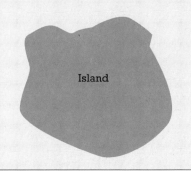

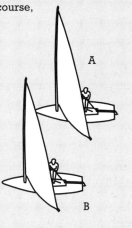

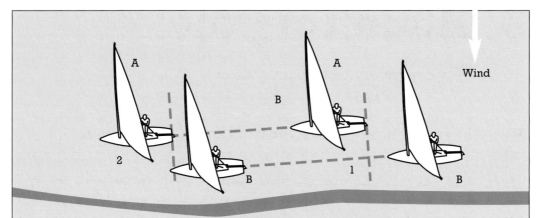

Continuing obstruction (e.g. river bank)

In position 1, B is about to get an overlap between A and the continuing obstruction.

Just as in the situation at the top of page 55, at the moment the overlap is established there is insufficient room for B to pass between A and the continuing obstruction, so B has no right to room. (Rule 18.5)

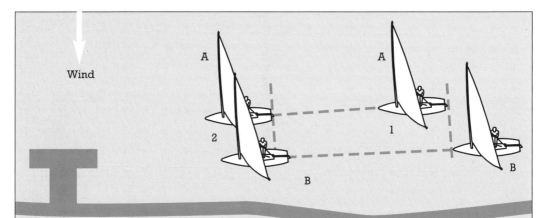

Continuing obstruction (e.g. river bank)

In position 1, B is about to get an overlap between A and the continuing obstruction.

Unlike the situation at the top of the page, at the moment the overlap is established there is sufficient room for B to pass between A and the continuing obstruction, so B has the right to room. (Rule 18.5)

At position 2, A will need to luff to give room to B, to allow B to get round the jetty. (Rules 18.5 & 18.2(a))

9 Rounding the Wing Mark

When the inside boat has to gybe to sail his proper course

Boat B has an undisputed overlap when the leading boat comes within two lengths. They will be gybing round the mark.

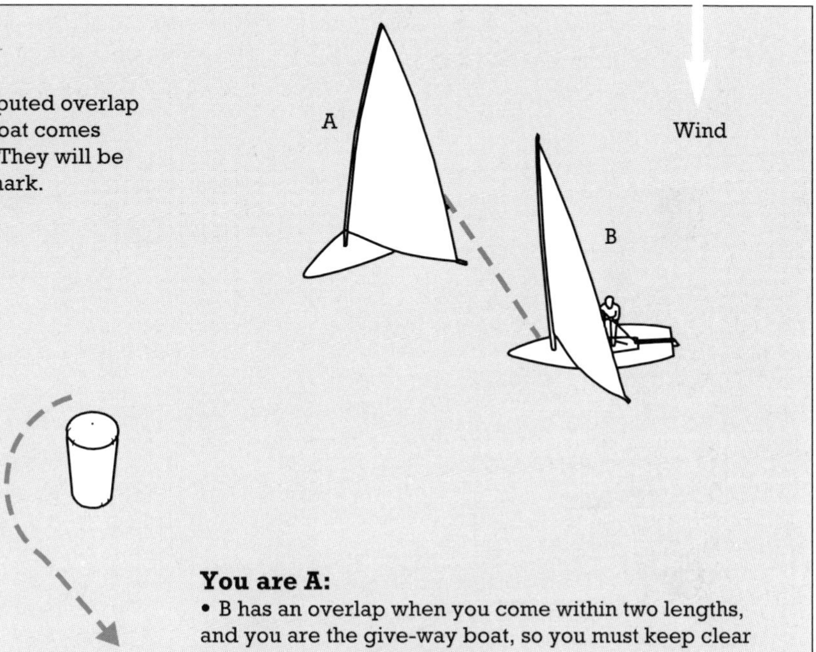

A

Wind

B

You are A:
• B has an overlap when you come within two lengths, and you are the give-way boat, so you must keep clear and give room. (Rule 18.2(a))

• If you now get clear ahead, you must continue to give room until B has rounded or passed the mark (that is, left it astern). You might do this by staying ahead, but if B is forced to change course to avoid you before he has left the mark astern, you will have broken a rule. (Rule 18.2(b))

You are B:
• Even if you have luffing rights, (for example if you were more than two lengths away from A when you became overlapped) then because your proper course is to gybe, as soon as you are 'about to round or pass' the mark (which is usually about three boat lengths), you must sail no higher than your proper course. (Rule 18.4)

• As A is overlapped outside you, you must gybe no later than you would have done had A not been there. (If it's very windy and you want to do a loop and tack instead of gybing, you will have to slow down and let A go ahead.) (Rule 18.4)

• After you have both gybed round the mark, and the mark is 'passed' (left clear astern with no chance of hitting it), then if you are overlapped, you will be the windward boat, and you must keep clear of A. A will have luffing rights. (Rule 11)

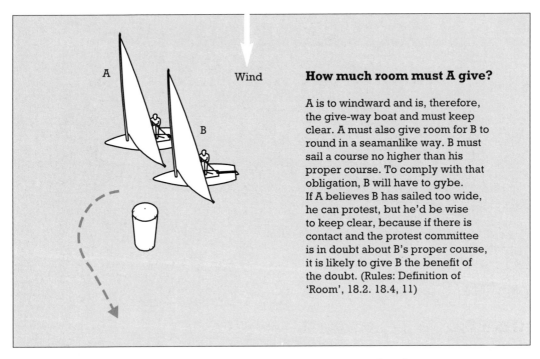

How much room must A give?

A is to windward and is, therefore, the give-way boat and must keep clear. A must also give room for B to round in a seamanlike way. B must sail a course no higher than his proper course. To comply with that obligation, B will have to gybe. If A believes B has sailed too wide, he can protest, but he'd be wise to keep clear, because if there is contact and the protest committee is in doubt about B's proper course, it is likely to give B the benefit of the doubt. (Rules: Definition of 'Room', 18.2. 18.4, 11)

When the inside boat does not have to gybe to sail his proper course

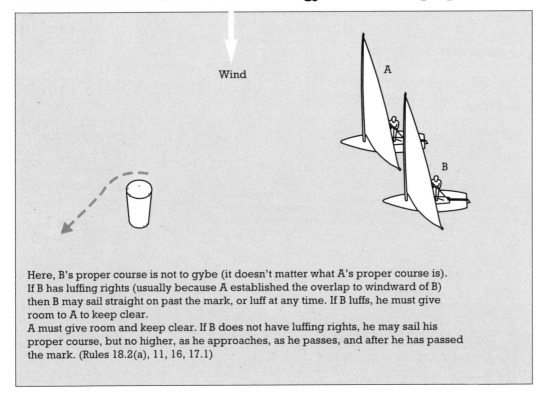

Here, B's proper course is not to gybe (it doesn't matter what A's proper course is). If B has luffing rights (usually because A established the overlap to windward of B) then B may sail straight on past the mark, or luff at any time. If B luffs, he must give room to A to keep clear.

A must give room and keep clear. If B does not have luffing rights, he may sail his proper course, but no higher, as he approaches, as he passes, and after he has passed the mark. (Rules 18.2(a), 11, 16, 17.1)

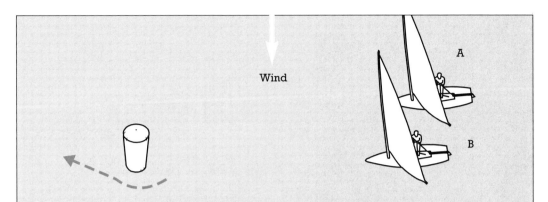

Here A, the give-way boat, will be on the inside. As soon as the boats are 'about to pass' the mark, B must start giving room, whether or not he has luffing rights. Room is 'the space a boat needs in the existing conditions while manoeuvring promptly in a seamanlike way'. A must keep clear of B.

When both boats have passed the mark (left it astern with no risk of hitting it), B may return to his proper course, or, if he has luffing rights, may sail as high as he likes, but must give A room to keep clear. (Rules 18.2(a), 11, 16, 17.1)

When there is doubt about the overlap

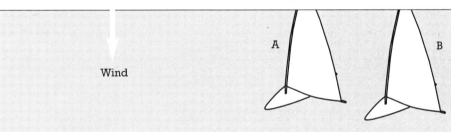

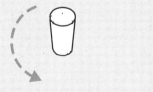

Often there is doubt whether or not there is an overlap at that critical moment when the leading boat reaches 'the zone' (two hull-lengths from the mark). It is easy to draw a picture in a book, or place models carefully on the protest room table, but in real life the moment passes in an instant. If you are flying a spinnaker and you're preparing for a gybe you'll be reluctant to spare anyone to go to the bow or stern to see if there's an overlap. In addition to knowing whether the boats are overlapped, it is difficult to judge when the leading boat is two hull lengths from the mark. Before you know it, the moment is gone, and the boats are converging towards the mark with the crew of one boat shouting 'no room' and the crew from the other shouting 'water', usually mixed with a fair number of unprintable words and phrases to give emphasis to their respective opinions.

In this diagram, who can say without the use of measuring instruments whether B has an overlap, and whether A is two lengths from the mark? If A luffs a little at the critical moment as he is just about to get to two boat lengths, maybe he could break an overlap. If this was happening on the water with boats that are moving rather than being frozen in a picture, and the overlap is in doubt, then the answer to the question 'must A give room to B?' depends on what was happening before they got to this position: see the next two diagrams.

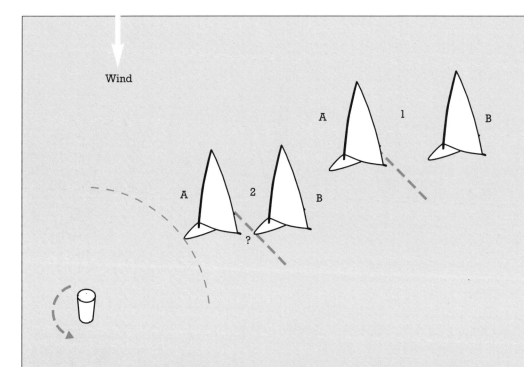

At position 1 there is no doubt that A is clear ahead. So at position 2, when there is doubt, it is resolved in A's favour. If B surges forward on a wave, A should keep clear and protest. If the water is flat, A could hail something like 'no water' and hold his proper course for the mark. B would be wise to slow down and follow A. There is no obligation on A to give room just because B is claiming he has the right to room. On the other hand, both boats are, of course, required to try to avoid contact. (Rules 18.2(e) & 14)

You are A:
Unless it is obvious that there is no overlap and B will not get one, try to get B's agreement that you are clear ahead well before your bow reaches the two hull-length zone. At least hail 'no overlap' well before you get to the critical 'two-lengths' position. If B subsequently claims that he got an inside overlap, the onus will be on him to establish that it was made in proper time. (Rules 18.2(c) & (e))

Your hail does not in itself place any obligation on B but will usually avoid a disagreement, a protest and (sometimes) damage.

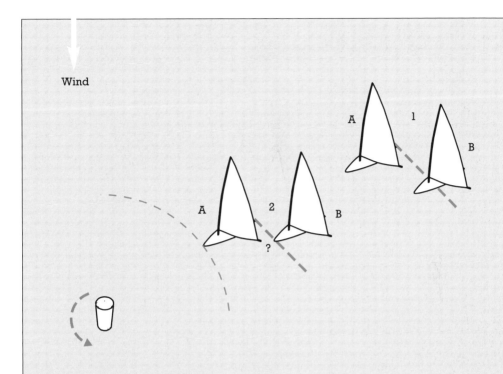

Here, at position 1 there is no doubt that B has an overlap. So when there is doubt at position 2, it is resolved in B's favour. Even if A surges forward on a wave and gets clear ahead at around two lengths, A must keep clear and give room. Both boats are, of course, required to try to avoid contact.

You are B:

Unless it is obvious that there is an overlap and A will not draw ahead and break it, try to get A's agreement that you have an overlap well before you reach the critical two hull-lengths zone. At least hail 'overlap' before you get to the 'two-lengths' position. If there is a protest and A claims that he subsequently broke the overlap, any doubt will be resolved in your favour. (Rules 18.2(b) & (e))

Your hail does not in itself place any obligation on A, but will usually avoid a disagreement, a protest and (sometimes) damage.

10 Rounding the Leeward Mark from the Reach

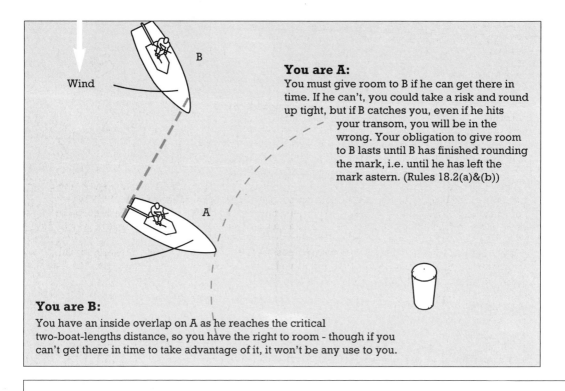

You are A:
You must give room to B if he can get there in time. If he can't, you could take a risk and round up tight, but if B catches you, even if he hits your transom, you will be in the wrong. Your obligation to give room to B lasts until B has finished rounding the mark, i.e. until he has left the mark astern. (Rules 18.2(a)&(b))

You are B:
You have an inside overlap on A as he reaches the critical two-boat-lengths distance, so you have the right to room - though if you can't get there in time to take advantage of it, it won't be any use to you.

You are A:
• At position 1, you're not 'about to round or pass' the mark, so:
  • If you have luffing rights you may luff and take B to windward of the mark if you want to, but if you change course you must give him room to keep clear, and if you reach a position where you are about to pass the mark (probably three hull-lengths from the mark, could be more, and very rarely less than two), then you must immediately give room if B is still overlapped. (Rules 11, 16, 18.1 & 18.2(a))
  • If you don't have luffing rights, you must not sail above your proper course. (Rule 17.1)

• Whether or not you have luffing rights, when you reach a point at which you are 'about to pass the mark' (about position 2) you must ignore your proper course and begin to bear away if necessary to give room. This is often more than two lengths from the mark. (Rules 18.1 & 18.2(a))

• Room is the 'space a boat needs in the existing conditions while manoeuvring promptly in a

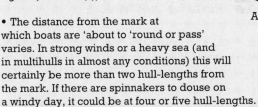

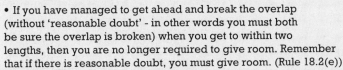

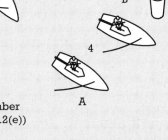

seamanlike way'. This usually means you will have to begin to bear away before you get to the critical two boat-lengths distance. As soon as the boats are 'about to pass' the mark you must start giving room, whether or not you have luffing rights. (Rule 18.2(a))

Wind

• The distance from the mark at which boats are 'about to 'round or pass' varies. In strong winds or a heavy sea (and in multihulls in almost any conditions) this will certainly be more than two hull-lengths from the mark. If there are spinnakers to douse on a windy day, it could be at four or five hull-lengths.

• If you have managed to get ahead and break the overlap (without 'reasonable doubt' - in other words you must both be sure the overlap is broken) when you get to within two lengths, then you are no longer required to give room. Remember that if there is reasonable doubt, you must give room. (Rule 18.2(e))

• From a tactical point of view, it may be better to slow down, let B go ahead, and tighten up round the mark immediately behind B, to prevent yourself getting trapped down to leeward of him as you come away from the mark. However, bear in mind that once B breaks the overlap, he is no longer limited to rounding in a 'seamanlike manner', and may sail wide and come up hard on the mark.

• If you are still overlapped when the mark is passed (left astern with no risk of hitting it), you may return to your proper course or, if you have luffing rights, may sail as high as you like, but you must give B room to keep clear. (Rule 16)

You are B:
• As you approach the mark, your obligation is to keep clear of A. (Rule 11)

• If A has luffing rights, he may luff you to windward of the mark, but he must stay outside a distance in which either of you would be 'about to round or pass' the mark. (Rule 18.1)

• When you are 'about to round or pass' the mark, you have the right to room to round inside A. Although 'room' does not mean that you can sail the course you might like to sail in the absence of A (what might be called a 'tactical' rounding) don't be intimidated by A trying to squeeze you right to the mark. If there is doubt in a protest, it is likely that A would be found not to have given sufficient room. If he doesn't give you enough room, it makes no difference whether you collide with the mark or the boat; whatever you hit (or if you hit both or even neither), if you feel you weren't given sufficient room, protest and sail on. (Rules 18.2(a), 28.1 & 31.3)

• Although A must give room, you remain the give-way boat and you must keep clear. When you have passed the mark (left it astern), A may luff to close-hauled (or his proper course if the next leg is a reach) and if he has luffing rights (can you remember how the overlap was established on the last leg?) A may luff and you must keep clear. (Rule 11)

When there is doubt about the overlap
See pages 60 and 61. The same principles apply here.

11 On the Run

All of Chapter 8 (On the Reach) applies equally on the run, but there are some additional situations which relate to boats on opposite tacks, and when one or both gybe.

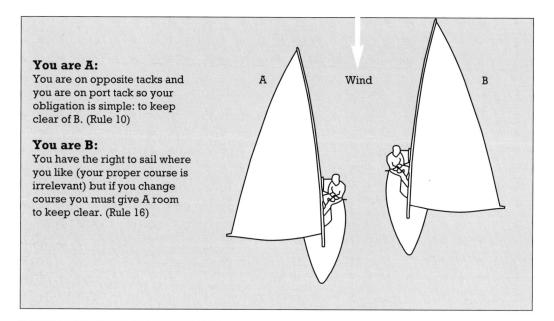

You are A:
You are on opposite tacks and you are on port tack so your obligation is simple: to keep clear of B. (Rule 10)

You are B:
You have the right to sail where you like (your proper course is irrelevant) but if you change course you must give A room to keep clear. (Rule 16)

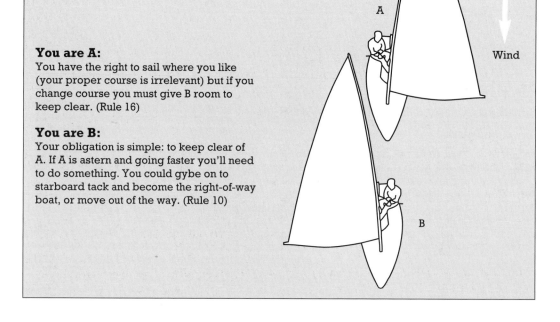

You are A:
You have the right to sail where you like (your proper course is irrelevant) but if you change course you must give B room to keep clear. (Rule 16)

You are B:
Your obligation is simple: to keep clear of A. If A is astern and going faster you'll need to do something. You could gybe on to starboard tack and become the right-of-way boat, or move out of the way. (Rule 10)

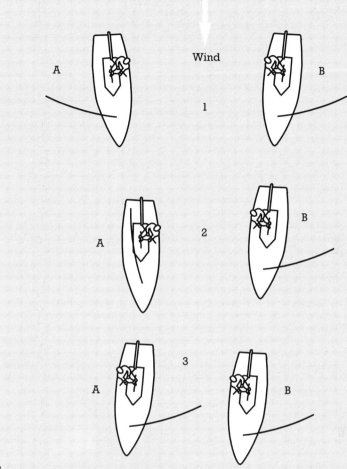

You are A:
• At position 1 you're on port tack and must keep clear. (Rule 10)

• At position 2 you are gybing into a 'give-way' position and your obligation to keep clear continues. (Rule 11)

• At position 3 you are windward boat and still required to keep clear. (Rule 11)

You are B:
• In position 1 you are the right-of-way boat, and may sail any course, but if you change course you must give A room to keep clear. (Rules 10 and 16)

• While A is gybing at position 2, you continue to be right-of-way boat, but if you change course you must give A room to keep clear. (Rules 10, 11 and 16)

• You have luffing rights as soon as A's mainsail fills on the new side, so you may continue to sail any course, but if you change course you must give A room to keep clear. (Rules 11 and 16)

In short, you are the right of way boat throughout, but if you change course you must give A room to keep clear. (Rules 10, 11 and 16)

You are A:
• At position 1 you're the right-of-way boat and may luff up to your proper course. If you've got luffing rights, you may luff as high as you like provided you give B room to keep clear. (Rules 11, 16 and 17.1)

• As soon as B's mainsail flips to fill on the port side (which means he's on starboard tack) you become the give-way boat and if you are on a collision course, as you are in position 2, you must do something to keep clear. (Rule 10)

You are B:
• At position 1 you are windward boat so you must keep clear. (Rule 11).

• From the moment you gybe you become the right-of-way boat, but you must gybe into a position which initially gives A room to keep clear, and if you change course you must give A room to keep clear. (Rules 15 & 16)

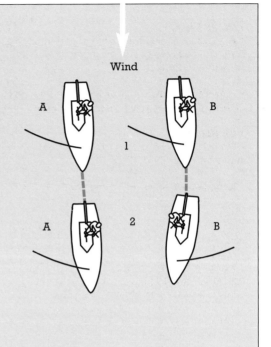

You are A:
• In position 1 you are the right-of-way boat, and may sail up to your proper course if you don't have luffing rights, and as high as you like if you do, but if you change course you must give B room to keep clear. (Rules 11 and 16)

• At position 2 you have gybed without changing course and you continue to be the right-of-way boat. As you did not change course you are not required to give B room to keep clear, but as I explained in Chapter 1, everyone must avoid contact if reasonably possible, so if your boom is going to make contact with B's boom, you should restrain it and protest. However, if there is contact with no damage, you cannot be penalised. (Rule 14)

You are B:
• At position 1 you're to windward and must keep clear. (Rule 11)

• It is wise to leave sufficient room for A to gybe, because if he does, you'll continue to be the give-way boat. (Rule 10)

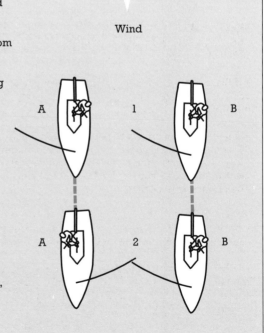

You are A:
• At position 1 you're the right-of-way boat, but if you change course you must give B room to keep clear. (Rules 10 & 16)

• At position 2 when B gybes you become the give-way boat and must keep clear. (Rule 11)

You are B:
• In position 1 you are the give-way boat, and must keep clear. (Rule 10)

• At position 2, when you gybe, you become the right-of-way boat, but A doesn't have to anticipate your being there, and there must be room for him to keep clear when you complete your gybe. (Rule 15)

• You may sail any course (you have luffing rights) but if you change course, you must give A room to keep clear. (Rule 16)

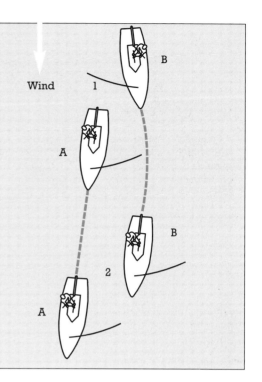

Passing a continuing obstruction

You are A:
You are on starboard tack, and B is on port tack, and you are gaining on him.

• If there is not room for you to pass between B and the continuing obstruction, you must keep clear of B. (Rule 18.5)

• If there is room for you to pass between B and the continuing obstruction at the moment you get an inside overlap, then you may sail between B and the shore and you remain the right-of-way boat. (Rules 10 & 18.5)

You are B:
• If there is not room for A to pass between you and the continuing obstruction, you are the right-of-way boat. (Rule 18.5)

• If there is room for A to pass between you and the continuing obstruction, then you remain the give-way boat and must keep clear, whether or not A is overlapped. This is true even if your draft is greater than A's and you can't get closer to the shore. (Rules 10 and 18.5)

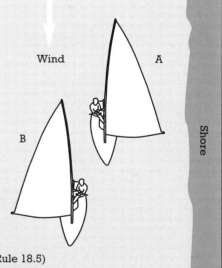

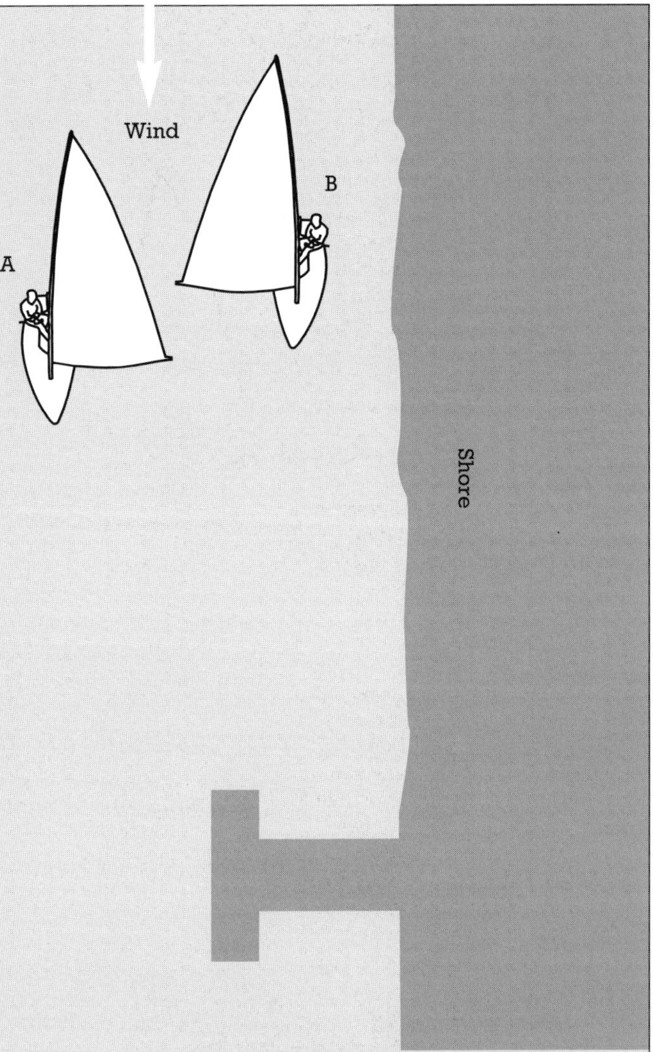

Wind

A

B

Shore

You are A:

• Your proper course is irrelevant. You may change course towards B, but only in such a way that B is able to keep clear. (Rule 16)

• Once B cannot, with safety, get any closer to the shore, then you must give him room to sail along between you and the shore. (Rule 18.2(a))

• If something sticks out from the shore ahead of B, you'll have to sail out to give B room to pass round it. (Rule 18.2(a))

• If B gybes, you become the windward boat and must keep clear. (Rule 11)

You are B:

• You must keep clear. When you cannot safely get any closer to the shore, then you may sail along the shoreline (or, more exactly, along the line that is safely close to the shore); A must give you room to do that. (Rules 10 & 18.2(a))

• There is no requirement to hail if you think he is pushing you too close for safety, but there is no other way he is to know that you think things are getting unsafe, so hail for room when you need it.

• If there is a danger projecting from the shore ahead (or if you think there is) A must give you room to come out round it; again it is advisable, though not essential, to hail for room. (Rule 18.2(a))

• If you gybe, you become the right-of-way boat with luffing rights so you may luff above your proper course if you want to, but if you change course you must give A room to keep clear. (Rules 11 and 16)

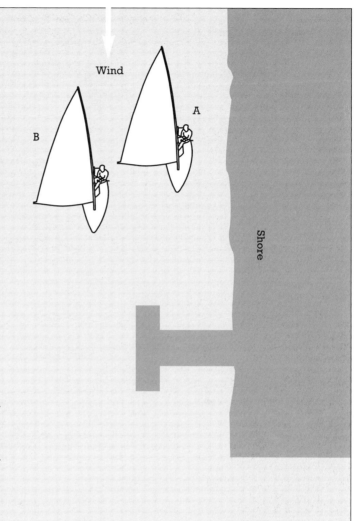

You are A:

• You must keep clear. When you cannot safely get any closer to the shore, then you may sail along the shoreline (or, more exactly, along the line that is safely close to the shore); B must give you room to do that. (Rules 11 & 18.2(a))

• There is no requirement to hail if you think he is pushing you too close for safety, but there is no other way he is to know that you think things are getting unsafe, so hail for room when you need it.

• If there is a danger projecting from the shore ahead (or if you think there is) B must give you room to come out round it; again it is advisable though not essential to hail for room. (Rule 18.2(a))

You are B:

• If you have luffing rights and A is some distance from the shore or obstruction, you may luff, but if you change course you must give him room to keep clear. (Rules 11 and 16)

• When the shore (or other obstruction) impedes A's ability to respond then you must stop luffing and bear away as is necessary to give him room. If he needs more room to come out round a projection, then you must give him room to do so. (Rule 18.2(a))

• If you don't have luffing rights, you may luff (in such a way that A can keep clear), up to your proper course. If your proper course is close to the shore, then you may force A towards the shore but must give A room when he gets there, as described in the last paragraph. (Rule 18.2(a))

12 Rounding the Leeward Mark from the Run

When the mark is a long way off, A, on port tack, would have to keep clear of B on starboard tack. On the other hand, if they were close to the mark, A has the right to room to round or pass the mark. The mark-rounding rules come into effect when the boats are 'about to round or pass' the mark. Under normal conditions, boats will have reached the 'about to round or pass' position at two hull lengths at the latest. When boats are lowering spinnakers in windy conditions with a tidal stream under them, they may be 'about to round or pass' at six or more hull lengths. On a river when boats are hardly making way against an adverse current, they may not be about to round or pass till they are less than two hull lengths from the mark.

At position 1, the boats are just reaching that critical position when they may be 'about to round or pass' the mark:

You are A:
* At position 1, you are on port tack so you must keep clear. In this situation you have little choice but to gybe. If you think you are about to round or pass, it would be best to shout this claim to B as he approaches. If he doesn't begin to give you room, keep clear and protest. (Rules 10, 18.1 & 18.2(a))

* At position 2 when you complete your gybe you are overlapped, so B has luffing rights, and you must keep clear. If you are not 'about to round or pass', he can sail you as far as he likes the wrong side of the mark. If you are 'about to round or pass the mark' then B must give you room. If you think you are 'about to round or pass', keep clear and protest. (Rules 11, 18.1 & 18.2(a))

* If you break the overlap (you could luff at position 2) then you become the right-of-way boat, but you can't just gybe in front of B, because as soon as you bear away you'll establish an overlap and be windward boat. (Rule 11)

* If after luffing to break the overlap at position 2, you bear away so that B is overlapped again, he doesn't have luffing rights and must not sail higher than his proper course. His proper course (the course he would sail if you weren't there) would be to gybe, so he must gybe. (Rule 17.1)

* If either of you get close enough to the mark that you are 'about to round or pass' then B must give you room. Room will include the space for two gybes. (Rule 18.2(a))

You are B:

• Position 1: Not to begin to give room at this position when A is claiming room leaves you open to protest and possible disqualification. If you are really going to take A the wrong side of the mark (rarely a good tactic when other boats are going to overtake you both), there has to be no doubt that you are not 'about to round or pass the mark'. But if these were Lasers on flat water with no tidal stream, you'd not be 'about to round or pass' at position 1. (Rule 18.1)

• If there is no doubt that you are not 'about to round or pass' the mark, then you may sail any course, but if you change course you must give A room to keep clear. (Rules 10 & 16)

• When A gybes at position 2, nothing changes. If there is no doubt that you are not 'about to round or pass' the mark, then you may sail any course, but if you change course you must give A room to keep clear. (Rules 11 & 16)

• If the overlap is broken at position 3 you become the give-way boat, but you may sail any course. (Rule 12)

• If the overlap is re-established, although you are the right-of-way boat, you must sail no higher than your proper course, gybing if necessary. (Rule 17.1)

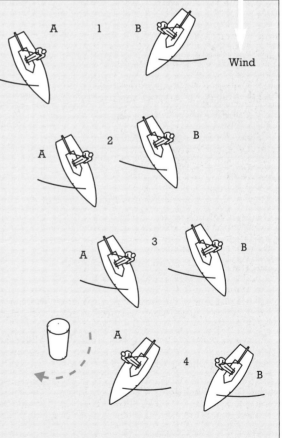

Now let's go back to the approach, and assume the boats are 'about to round or pass' the mark.

You are A:

• At position 1, you are overlapping on the inside. Even though you have not yet reached the two hull-lengths zone, B may have to start giving you room. (Rule 18.2(a))

• You must keep clear of B, while B gybes (Rule 10)

• At position 3, even though you are the right-of-way boat with luffing rights, you may not sail B past the mark. You must gybe no later than the position at which you would have gybed to sail your proper course round the mark in the absence of B. B must give you room to gybe. (Rules 18.2(a) & 18.4).

• When you have gybed, if you are still overlapped as you are in position 4, you become the give-way boat and must keep clear of B, but B must give you room to round the mark. (Rules 11 & 18.2(a))

• When you have left the mark astern, then if you are still overlapped, you must continue to keep clear. B has luffing rights and may sail higher than his close-hauled course. (Rules 11, 18.1 & 18.2(a))

You are B:

• Position 1: Because A has an overlap as you become 'about to round or pass' the mark, you may have to start giving room before you reach the two hull-lengths zone. In this diagram, you will need to gybe at position 1. (Rule 18.2(a))

• After gybing at position 2, you become the give-way boat and you must keep clear. (Rule 11)

• A must not sail above his proper course, so at position 4 he must gybe. If he doesn't, you may protest, but you should still keep clear. (Rule 11)

• When A gybes at position 4, and you gybe, you become the right-of-way boat with luffing rights, but you must give room to A to round the mark in a seamanlike way. If he takes too much room, it is best to give it to him and protest. Then you can't lose the protest; if the protest committee finds he took too much room, he'll be disqualified, and if it finds he didn't, neither boat will be penalised. (Rule 18.2(a))

• Soon after position 4, it is best to drop astern and round up tight to the mark, rather than be left in A's windshadow. However, if you are still overlapped when both boats have completed the rounding (that is, left the mark astern), then as you have luffing rights you may luff as high as you like, but you must give A room to keep clear. (Rules 11 & 16)

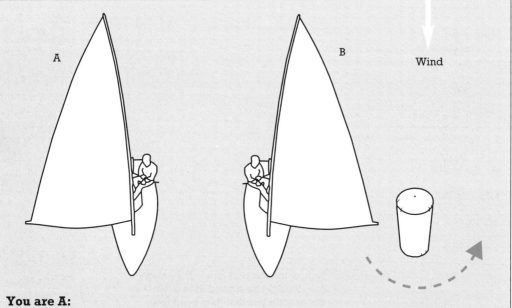

You are A:
• You must keep clear of B. (Rule 10)

• B must not sail above his proper course, so he must gybe. If he doesn't, it's best to continue to keep clear, and protest. (Rules 10 & 18.4)

You are B:
• Until you were 'about to round or pass the mark', you could sail where you liked, but if you changed course you had to give A room to keep clear. (Rule 16)

• Now you are 'about to round or pass the mark' you must sail no higher than your proper course. This will mean gybing of course (you can't sail straight on even though you are on starboard tack and A is on port tack). (Rule 18.4)

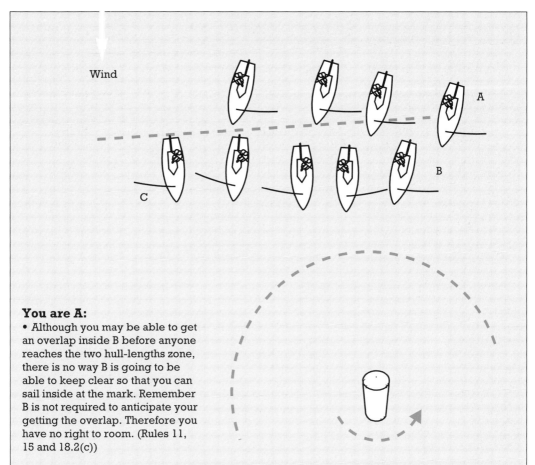

You are A:

• Although you may be able to get an overlap inside B before anyone reaches the two hull-lengths zone, there is no way B is going to be able to keep clear so that you can sail inside at the mark. Remember B is not required to anticipate your getting the overlap. Therefore you have no right to room. (Rules 11, 15 and 18.2(c))

• You do have an overlap, without doubt, on the inside of C and, unlike B, C is able to give room. C therefore must keep clear if you maintain the overlap to the two hull-lengths zone. (Rules 18.2(a) & 10)

You are B:

• As you've had the overlap for some time, those boats outside must keep clear (either because they are to windward on the same tack, or are on port tack). They might need to start giving you room before the two hull-lengths zone. It might be a good idea to tell A that it's too late for him to get an overlap now, and tell the boats outside you that they need to start giving you room now. (Rules 10, 11 & 18.2(a))

• If they don't keep clear, try to get the correct side of the mark, even if it means colliding with the mark or the boat outside you (providing there is no damage). If you are forced the wrong side of the mark you might succeed with a protest but you cannot recover the places lost. (Rules 62.1(b) & 14)

You are C:

• This is not a good place to be! A has an inside overlap, and you are able to keep clear, so keep clear you must, as well as keeping clear of all the boats inside you. Next time, don't get into this position! (Rules 10 & 18.2(a))

13 The Finish

You finish when any part of your hull, crew or equipment first touches the finishing line, from the direction of the last mark. Typically, the first part of the boat to cross the line is the stem, but your crew's hand held over his head when he's out on the trapeze would count if that was his 'normal position'.

With a downwind finish, the spinnaker is usually the first piece of equipment to cross the line. If the spinnaker head was let out a few centimetres, and the boat often sailed with it like that, that would be OK, but a spinnaker with its head let go several metres would not count, because it would not be in its normal position (whether this had been done intentionally or not). A boat that had let its spinnaker go would be finished on the first piece of the boat to cross the line that was not out of position - probably its stem or pulpit.

You are 'racing' until you have cleared the finishing line and the finishing marks. You have cleared the line when no part of your boat or its equipment is straddling the line. You have

cleared the finishing marks when you are first in a position that is not in danger of making contact with a mark. The usual way of doing this is just to keep sailing right over the line near the middle (which would mean you are clear of the marks) or, if you finish near an end, to sail right through the line and get clear of the mark.

You don't have to cross the line completely; having finished with the first part of the boat or its equipment touching the line, you can duck back on to the course side of the line if you want to.

When you have finished and cleared the line, you are still subject to the racing rules, but you cannot be penalised (so there is no need to take a penalty) for infringing a 'when boats meet' rule (unless you interfere with a boat that is still racing). (Rules: Part 2 Preamble and 22.1)

If you have not sailed the correct course, once you have finished you cannot go back and complete the course, because as soon as you have finished and cleared the line and marks, you are no longer 'racing'.

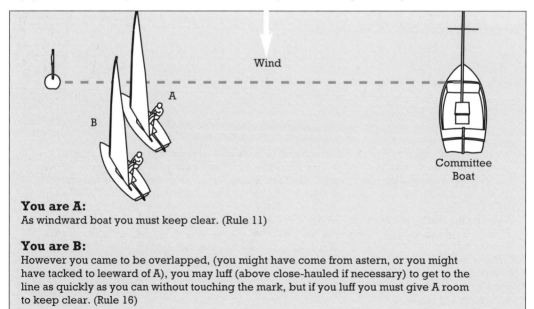

You are A:
As windward boat you must keep clear. (Rule 11)

You are B:
However you came to be overlapped, (you might have come from astern, or you might have tacked to leeward of A), you may luff (above close-hauled if necessary) to get to the line as quickly as you can without touching the mark, but if you luff you must give A room to keep clear. (Rule 16)

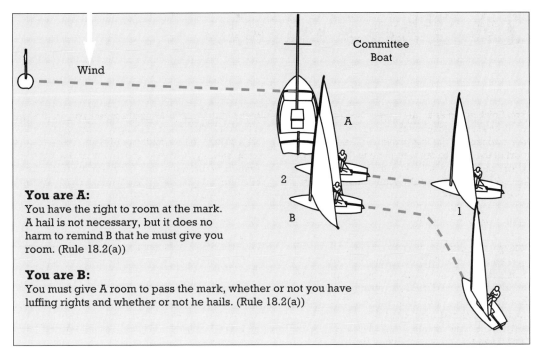

You are A:
You have the right to room at the mark. A hail is not necessary, but it does no harm to remind B that he must give you room. (Rule 18.2(a))

You are B:
You must give A room to pass the mark, whether or not you have luffing rights and whether or not he hails. (Rule 18.2(a))

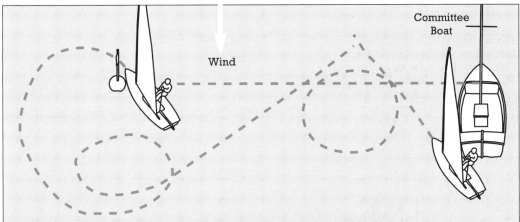

If, before finishing, you touch a finishing mark (a buoy or the committee boat) you must sail clear of other boats and do a 360 penalty including a tack and a gybe (it doesn't matter which comes first). You must then sail to where you are wholly on the course side of the line, and finish. (Rule 31.2)

If you hit the mark after finishing but before clearing the line and the mark, you 'unfinish' yourself when you hit it. You must sail clear of other boats and do a 360 penalty, sail to where you are wholly on the course side of the line, and then finish again. (Rule 31.2)

You don't have to be clear of the line when you do the 360 (you can be straddling it or on the post-finish side of it), but if, having taken the penalty, you are not on the course side, you must go back to the course side, and then finish. (Rule 31.2)

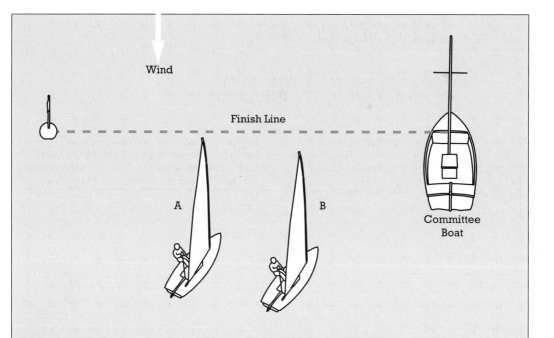

You are A:

As windward boat you must keep clear of B, even if B luffs. Whether or not he has luffing rights, B has the right to luff to head-to-wind to finish as quickly as he can. (Rules 11, 17.1 definition of 'proper course')

If B hails for room to tack, you have to make a quick judgement as to whether you can fetch the committee boat on this tack. To 'fetch' means to pass without tacking, so you can luff to head-to-wind but you must get past the bow of the committee boat without going through head-to-wind. If you can, you can refuse room (you should hail a refusal such as 'no room') but if you refuse room and then cannot fetch the committee boat, you'll have to do a 720-degree penalty before you can be recorded as having finished. (Rule 19.2)

If you cannot lay the committee boat, you must either:

1. Tack, or

2. Hail back 'you tack' and take on the responsibility of giving room to B
(typically by ducking B's stern as he tacks).

You are B:

Because of the obstruction ahead, you may hail A for room to tack. If A refuses to tack or otherwise give room, you may 'shoot' the line; that is, sail head-to-wind and hope you will have sufficient way for your bow to touch the line - that's all you need! If A refuses to respond to your hail, slow and tack under his stern. If he fails to fetch the committee boat without tacking, you may protest him if he doesn't take a penalty. (Rule 19)

If A responds to your hail by tacking, you must tack as soon as possible. (Rule 19.1(a))

If A responds to your hail by hailing 'you tack', you must tack. (Rule 19.1(b))

14 Means of Propulsion

You must not 'increase, maintain or decrease' the speed of your boat by any means other than by using 'wind and water'. At major dinghy championships the sailing instructions often allow the jury to penalise boats it sees infringing the propulsion rule, without a hearing. Often, jury members go afloat and protest boats they believe are breaking the rule. (Rules 42 & 67)

The differential in speed between a dinghy complying with the propulsion rule and one propelled illegally by a skilled crew paying no attention to it can, in very light winds, be so enormous that in a half-knot zephyr the complying boat wouldn't have reached the windward mark when the infringing boat had completed the course, travelling six times as fast. (Rule 42)

The difference lessens as the wind speed increases, but can still be significant in a competitive fleet at a wind speed of 15 knots. Since the difference in boatspeed between top competitors in competitive dinghy fleets is often as little as one tenth of one per cent, breaking Rule 42 is an obvious attraction not only to the unscrupulous, but to the honest sailor when he sees less honest sailors 'getting away with it'.

So what does Rule 42 seek to control? If you rock a rig to windward in still air, the sail passing through the still air has the same effect as moving air passing over a still sail: a driving force is set up. The same sort of effect, though not quite as effective, can be obtained by hauling in the sail: the force drives the boat forward, and the rig or sail can be returned to 'leeward' ready for another go. Waggling the tiller can also drive a hull through calm water. Moving the trunk of the body forward and backwards, even in strong winds, can flap the leech and increase the sail's drive.

With practice one can become very efficient at driving a boat through the water on a calm day; it's really quite fun, though very energetic. There is a minority of dinghy sailors who would prefer that there were no restrictions (i.e. most of the prohibitions in Rule 42 were removed as they are for boardsailing (see Appendix B)). Removing the propulsion restrictions would certainly make life easier for race committees and juries, since the rule is not easy to enforce. However, the vast majority of good sailors do not want 'kinetics' (imparting energy from moving crew weight into forward motion) to be part of sailing. Attitudes might change; up to a few years ago, board sailors did not want to allow kinetics, now they do, resulting in only very fit and strong people being able to win boardsailing championships.

At championships, and at well-organised regional regattas, a jury goes afloat to look for offenders; a good race committee will also not hesitate to take action. However, this should not change your policy; if you see someone pumping, rocking or sculling, you should protest, and not break the rule yourself.

15 Taking a Penalty

When and where to take a penalty

When you know you've broken a rule or a sailing instruction, you must take a penalty or retire promptly from the race, unless the rule or sailing instruction broken is one which requires you do something while racing, and you were not racing at the time of the incident (i.e. it occurred before the preparatory signal or after you finish and clear the finishing line). In such a case you do not have to take a penalty (but if you've caused damage you may have to pay for the repair).

If you are racing and you break a 'when boats meet' rule, you must take a 720 penalty promptly. Let's suppose you are sailing up the first beat, and you are close-hauled on port tack, chatting to your crew about tactics. Suddenly you are aware of a starboard tack boat bearing away under your stern. As he bears away under your stern he shouts something at you so you know he is aggrieved. What should you do? Tell him you're going to take a penalty, and immediately sail clear of other boats and do a 720. Actually, if he doesn't hail 'protest' he cannot protest, but that should not affect whether or not you take the penalty. If you know you have broken a rule, and the other guy is aggrieved, the paragraph called 'Sportsmanship and the Rules' at the beginning of the rulebook makes it clear that you must take the penalty. Not to do so could result in a protest under Rule 2 'Fair Sailing' or a report resulting in a 'Rule 69 hearing' against you for a 'gross breach of good sportsmanship'.

What if you did see him coming and when you were just about to tack, he shouted 'carry on'? You carry on on port tack and he bears away under your stern. Should you take a penalty? No. By accepting his invitation to carry on, and him ducking your stern, you have in fact kept clear. (By the way, the hail of 'carry on' did not compel you to sail on; you could have tacked if you had wanted to).

What if he bears away under your stern, but

says nothing. My recommendation is that if he shows no signs of being aggrieved, then you can assume you kept clear, but bear in mind that a protest against you lodged by a third boat witnessing the incident might succeed, but if the protestor is within hailing distance he has to hail to you that he's going to protest, in which case you can take your penalty if you think you've broken a rule.

If you touch a mark while racing, then you are honour-bound to take a 360-degree penalty, even if no one saw you. This is the test of a good sportsman. We all need to be good sportsmen if we are going to play this great game of fleet racing without the need for referees or judges. (Rule 31.2)

If you sail the wrong course, or propel the boat by means other than by the use of 'wind and water', or you are on the course side of the starting line at the starting signal, you cannot exonerate yourself by taking a penalty. However, you can often exonerate yourself by doing something else; if you realise before you finish that you've sailed the wrong course you can go and sail the right one (if you can do it within the time limit); if you've gone round a mark the wrong way, you can unwind yourself and go round it the right away; if you were a premature starter you can usually go back and start. But having pumped your way down the reaching leg, or paddled, or moored up to the shore for an ice-cream, or - heaven forbid - failed to rescue someone in distress, then there is no exoneration procedure open to you, and you must retire from the race immediately you realise you have broken the rule or sailing instruction.

Remember that if you want to take a 720 penalty after an incident in the preparatory period, or you hit a starting mark in the preparatory period, then you may (in fact you must) take the penalty as soon as you can, so if the infringement is some minutes before the start, you will not be disadvantaged.

If the infringement happens on or close to the

finishing line, then you must do the 720 as soon as possible (on either side of the finishing line or its extensions), and then cross the finishing line in the direction from the last mark. It is possible, therefore, to finish (when the first part of the boat touches the line), then break a rule of Part 2 before clearing the line (which has the effect of 'un-finishing'), do a 720, then come back wholly behind the line and 'refinish' when the first part of the boat touches the line again from the course side.

If you break a 'when boats meet' rule (for example by taking room at a mark to which you are not entitled) and you hit the mark, you can exonerate yourself by doing just a 720; you don't have to do the 360 for hitting the mark as well. If you have broken more than one rule in an incident, you need take only one 720 penalty.

How to take the penalty

The standard penalty for infringing a 'when boats meet' rule is the '720 degree turn', which is described in Rule 44. If there is nothing said about penalties in the sailing instructions, then the 720 penalty applies.

If you have room, do the penalty immediately (and it costs you nothing to tell the other guy you're going to do it). If there isn't room, tell the other guy you're going to do it, immediately sail to where there is room, or slow down to let the surrounding boats pass. Rotate your boat through two turns. Do the second turn immediately after the first, and make sure you finish pointing in the same direction that you were sailing when you started the turns. (If you're on a beat make sure you're not 90 degrees short.) Make sure you include two tacks and two gybes. When you are training, you should practice doings 720's so that you can do them as quickly as possible; there's no point in adding to the penalising effect by getting into

irons. When you practice 720's you'll realise that when you're on a beat, it's usually best to bear off first rather than tack. (Rule 44.2)

Sometimes sailing instructions replace the '720' penalty with a 'scoring' penalty system (usually for keelboat events in which it is thought unsafe for boats to be doing circles, or because they have different ratings). When the sailing instructions prescribe a 'scoring penalty' then instead of doing a 720, you must display a yellow flag and inform the race committee after the finish that you are taking a penalty. (Rule 44.3)

Protest, take a penalty, or both?

After the preparatory signal, if you are involved in an incident with another boat (or several other boats) in which you think a rule has, or may have, been broken, you have to make a decision and you have to make it quickly. If there has been a collision, however small or unavoidable, then almost certainly a rule will have been broken, and of course even without a collision there might have been an infringement.

If you know you have broken a rule but think the other boat has broken one too, you can protest and take a penalty. Hail 'protest', then sail clear and take the penalty.

If you have a collision, but were in the right or entitled to room, and there is no damage then you cannot be penalised. You can sail on. If there is damage (to either boat) which you could have avoided (though you need not act to avoid contact until it is clear that the other boat is not keeping clear or giving room), then you can do a 720 penalty to exonerate yourself. If the damage is serious, then you cannot exonerate yourself with a 720, and you must retire.

16 Protesting

Some people, even very experienced competitors, say they find protesting unpleasant. Protesting need not be done with any acrimony whatsoever, and unless we want to evolve a breed of referees to blow whistles and penalise on the spot (and there'll need to be lots of them all over the course, because under such a system no one will dream of taking a penalty if they don't hear a whistle) then we have to accept that the sport is policed by the following system:

When a competitor knows he has broken a rule he takes a penalty (or retires).

When a competitor thinks another competitor has broken a rule, and the other competitor doesn't retire or take a penalty, he protests.

When the race committee (or jury if there is one) sees a rule infringement which affects the fairness of the competition and the boat doesn't take a penalty, it protests.

In my opinion (though many judges will not agree with me) there is one other consideration that affects a decision as to whether or not a penalty should be taken or a protest made against another boat when a rule is broken. That is, whether or not the right-of-way boat (or the boat with the right to room) is aggrieved. You're on starboard tack a lap ahead of a beginner on port tack and you have to duck under his stern. There is nothing to be gained by protesting; a word over a beer after the race would be much more appropriate. Of course in this scenario there is no rule requiring you to protest. But what if you're the one on port tack and a rival ducks under your stern, but says nothing. As I said in the last chapter, I believe if he is not aggrieved, you can assume there's no infringement. That's the criteria I use when I'm racing. If he says even 'tut tut', I'll do a penalty if I think I've broken a rule. Sometimes I'm not sure if I have broken a rule. If the other guy thinks I have, that's usually enough for me, and I'll go and do my turns.

When you consider another boat has broken a rule and you feel aggrieved about it, you will want to protest. This chapter is about how to lodge a protest.

There are certain requirements that must be met before a protest can be accepted as valid, and a hearing opened. The only requirement you actually need to remember is the one which has to be met out there on the water; the rest you can look up in this book when you are back at the clubhouse.

Things to remember on the water

Any boat may protest, provided that the protesting boat was involved in or witnessed an incident. Even if you have been involved in a previous incident in which you will be disqualified (after a hearing), that doesn't remove your right to protest about a later incident. (ISAF Case 1)

The only thing you need to do at the time of the incident is to hail the word 'protest'. The rule says this must be done 'at the first reasonable opportunity'. So there is time to ask him whether he's going to take a penalty, and if he says 'no', hail 'protest'. If you get no reaction to the hail, it's best to repeat it more loudly.

If your hull length is 6 metres or more, you also need to display a protest flag, and this too must be done 'at the first reasonable opportunity'. Don't wait too long. Many protests have been found to be invalid because the flag was not displayed very soon after the incident. The flag must be red. It doesn't matter what the shape is, but it must be red, and it must be a flag, not a red glove or waterproof jacket. The usual flag is the code flag B which has swallowtails, but a rectangular red flag will do just as well. It must be displayed conspicuously which means it mustn't be too small, and it must be up in the rigging and not lying on the deck. It must be kept displayed until you finish, or if the incident is near the finishing line, until the race committee acknowledges seeing the flag (you can draw the committee's attention to it after finishing).

If the flag is already being displayed because of a previous incident, then that's fine; you don't have to pull it down and put it up again, or display another one.

The purpose of the hail and the flag is two-fold. It gives an opportunity for the protestee to take a penalty, and if he decides not to take a penalty, then it marks the moment so that he can recall what happened.

You cannot lodge a protest if you don't hail, but you don't have to go ahead and lodge the protest if you have hailed.

If the other man might not have heard your hail of 'protest' at the time of the incident you should inform him again at the next opportunity you get, even if the next opportunity is ashore.

Things to do when you come ashore

You need to fill in a protest form. If you can't find one, and unless there is some special sailing instruction (ugh!) any bit of paper will do provided that you include certain pieces of vital information. Most people make too much of filling in the form. By including too much detail, you're more likely to do yourself harm than good, and you'll certainly wear out the brain unnecessarily. Initially you need only identify the incident, but as you will need to include your identity (you are the protestor), and that of the protestee, the number of the rule broken, you may as well complete that initially if you can.

You need to lodge the form with the protest committee within the time limit (which is two hours after the last boat finishes unless otherwise specified in the sailing instructions). If there is a good reason for any delay, the protest committee must extend the time limit. (Rule 61.3)

Preparing your witnesses

If there is someone who you think saw the incident, approach him and, having simply identified the incident so that he knows what you're taking about, ask him what he saw. Don't tell him anything and don't ask leading questions. If you think what he saw is what you believe really happened, then ask him if he will be a witness at the hearing.

At the hearing, when you are invited to call witnesses, explain to the chairman that you have not discussed the case with your witness, you merely asked what he saw and considered that as this was more or less what actually happened, you thought he would be a good witness.

When your witness gives his evidence and is questioned, it will invariably become obvious to the protest committee that he has in no way been influenced, and his credibility and the value of his evidence will help you enormously. You'd do better with no witness at all than a 'coached' witness; their complicity is obvious to all but the most inexperienced protest committee.

Conducting yourself at the hearing

If you are an experienced racing skipper sailing in a minor event, there is a good chance that you will know more about the rules and procedures than the protest committee does. Use this knowledge carefully if you wish not to be disadvantaged. At any hearing you should treat the committee members (and indeed the other parties and witnesses) with respect. They are usually fellow sailors doing their best to be fair, but even when this is not the case, losing your cool gains you nothing.

The procedure

Appendix P of the racing rules, which gives a recommended procedure for protest committees, is very well written and easy to follow. Here is a summary.

The protestor and protestee are called to the hearing. You must both be present during all of the taking of evidence (from each of you, and of any witnesses called by you, by your opponent or by the protest committee). If one party chooses not to attend, then the protest committee can proceed without him.

The validity of the protest must be considered by the protest committee:

'Was a hail of 'Protest' made, and was it made at the first reasonable opportunity after the incident?' For boats over 6 metres: 'Was the protest flag displayed, and was it displayed at the first reasonable opportunity after the incident?' 'Was it conspicuously displayed?'

'Was it kept displayed till the finish?'

Was the written protest received in proper time?

Did the written protest identify the nature of the incident?

Although the protest committee must extend the time limit for receiving protests if there is a good reason for a delay, it has no power to excuse any of the other requirements, and if they are not met the protest must be found to be invalid, and refused. A protest committee cannot find as a fact that the protestor did not hail 'protest' and say 'We'll let you off this time, but don't forget for next time' and proceed to hear the protest.

If the protest is ruled as valid, the protest committee must proceed to the next stage: the hearing of evidence.

The protestor describes his version of the incident; the protestee then does likewise. Each may question the other and the protest committee members may question both. Each is invited to call witnesses, one at a time, and each witness describes his version of the incident, and is questioned by the parties (the protestor and the protestee) and the committee. The committee may call witnesses, or the committee members may themselves be witnesses in which case they give their evidence and may be questioned. The protestor summarises his case; the protestee summarises his defence.

The protest committee deliberates in private (if there were observers, they too are asked to leave) and produces 'facts found' (what it thinks happened), its decision and the grounds for that decision. The parties are then recalled and the chairman reads out the details.

17 Requesting Redress & Appealing

If you think your position in a race, or in a series, has been made significantly worse through no fault of your own, you can sometimes successfully 'request redress' (often erroneously called 'protesting the race committee'). Redress is usually in the form of points that the protest committee considers you would have been awarded had you finished without being prejudiced. (Rules 62, 64.2)

Unlike a protest (for which there are several validity requirements), it is rare for a request for redress to be refused on the grounds it is invalid. The only reason for refusal to hear a redress request would be that it was received after the closing time for receiving protests (usually two hours after the incident), without a good reason.

You can write your request on any bit of paper, but is usual to use a protest form even though many of the prompts are not relevant. For example, you don't have to display a protest flag, or make a hail.

So it is not difficult to get a hearing; being awarded redress is another matter! Generally the procedure at the hearing is the same as a protest hearing, except that if you are the only one requesting redress, you will take on the 'protestor's' role, and a representative of the race committee will usually act as the 'defendant'.

The protest committee should be independent of the race committee; if you think it isn't, raise the issue early in the proceedings. If the event is anything more than a club race, wise organisers will have appointed a jury that is independent of the race committee; at an international event there'll usually be an international jury. At club events the usual practice is for the race committee to arrange a protest committee as independent as is practical, if a request for redress is received by the race committee.

Like a protest hearing, there are the same distinct parts to the hearing: the taking of evidence (from you, your fellow redress requesters if there are

any, the race committee, and anyone else you, the race committee, or the protest committee sees fit to call); the assessment by the protest committee (sitting in private) as to whether redress is applicable; and lastly, if redress is applicable, what redress will be given.

Redress can be given to you only when:

• Your finishing position has been made significantly worse.

• You've done nothing wrong yourself. So if you have been scored 'OCS' ('on course side' for being over the line at the start), and are simply complaining that there were some boats ahead of you that were not scored OCS, you can't get redress. (You could protest the guilty boats, of course.)

• Your finishing position was affected for one of the following reasons:

(a) The race committee (or the protest committee) made an improper action or omission. So if some passing whale rammed you, you cannot get redress; a rescue boat would be another matter, as that would be under the control of the race committee. If the race committee fails to make a signal correctly and this affected you, you'd be entitled to redress. The race committee is not permitted to prejudice anyone's finishing position (in a race or series of races), whether or not it adheres to the rules and sailing instructions that govern its conduct.

For example, if the race committee writes itself a sailing instruction saying it can shorten course at any time for any reason, and it shortens course for no apparent reason just as your rival approaches the first mark after twenty minutes of racing - his father is the race officer - you would have a legitimate claim for redress. Conversely, if the sailing instructions said the first leg would be 3 kilometres long and it was only 2.5, it would be impossible to argue that any competitor had been prejudiced and so no redress could be given.

(b) You have been physically damaged by a boat required to keep clear or give room or by a vessel not racing that was required to keep clear of you (for example under the collision regulations). So if you're on starboard and a boat on port rams you, putting a hole in your side, and you have to retire, you can get redress. You can only get redress if you're damaged; if you simply got tangled up with this port tacker while some close rivals pass you, you cannot get redress. If at a mark you are entitled to room but not given it and forced the wrong side, you must return to round or pass the mark correctly, and although you may successfully protest the boat that didn't give you room, because you were not physically damaged you are not entitled to redress for the fifty places you may have lost.

(c) You went to help someone in distress. If you see someone in distress you are required to go to their aid, so if you lose places by your heroic act you are entitled to redress.

(d) You have been significantly affected by someone who is penalised (under Rule 69) for cheating, or infringing the 'Fair Sailing' rule.

The protest committee will hear your evidence and that of your witnesses, and if relevant the evidence and advice of the race committee. In private it will then 'find facts' and assess whether these facts meet the criteria for giving redress, and if they do, what redress is to be given.

If your request meets the above criteria, then you must be given redress. It is not unusual to be awarded points equal to a position the protest committee thinks you would have achieved had you not been prejudiced, or points equal to your 'average to date in the series' (perhaps not counting your 'discard'). In giving redress, the only restriction imposed on the protest committee is that its decision shall be as fair as possible to all boats affected. Faced with a complex situation, a protest committee may decide that the fairest arrangement is 'no adjustment to any finishing positions'. To abandon or cancel a race is rarely the fairest solution, although sometimes there is no alternative. (Rule 64.2)

Appealing

If you are penalised as a result of a hearing, you usually have the right to appeal against the protest committee's decision, but to be eligible you need to be a 'party' directly affected by the decision against which you are appealing. (Rules 70 & 71)

If you are indirectly affected, for instance, if you find yourself in a lower position as a result of the protest committee giving redress to another boat then you must first request redress on the grounds that the committee's action materially prejudiced your finishing position, and if you are not satisfied with that decision, you may appeal. You may also appeal against a decision not to hear your protest or your request for redress, or against the fairness of redress awarded as a result of your request.

Sometimes there is no right to appeal. You have no right to appeal:

• When, at an international event, an 'international jury' has been appointed, and it complies with the requirements of Appendix Q; or

• When 'it is essential to determine promptly the result of a race that will qualify a boat to compete in a later stage of an event or a subsequent event'. In the UK, the approval from the Royal Yachting Association is also required. In the USA, no approval is required from the USSA. In all cases, the fact that decisions are not open to appeal must be announced in the notice of the race and in the sailing instructions. (Rules 70.4(a) & Appendix M 1.2(11))

Unless the facts found by the protest committee are completely incompatible with all the evidence or with the protest committee's own diagram, you can appeal solely on a question of interpretation of the rules, and not against the facts found by the protest committee. (Rule 70.1)

The protest committee may itself refer a case it has decided for confirmation or correction. (Rule 70.1(b))

How to appeal

This varies from country to country, so look at Rule 70 and any prescription to the rule that your own national authority may have written.

The RACING RULES of SAILING for 2001–2004

INTRODUCTION

The Racing Rules of Sailing includes two main sections. The first, Parts 1–7, contains rules that affect all competitors. The second section contains appendices that provide details of rules, rules that apply to particular kinds of racing, and rules that affect only a small number of competitors or officials.

Revision The racing rules are revised and published every four years by the International Sailing Federation (ISAF), the international authority for the sport. This edition becomes effective on 1 April 2001. With the exception of Appendices 1, 2 and 3, changes to the racing rules are permitted under ISAF Regulations 11.2 and 11.3. No changes are contemplated before 2005, but any changes determined to be urgent before then will be announced through national authorities and posted on the ISAF website (www.sailing.org).

ISAF Codes New appendices 1, 2 and 3 contain the ISAF Advertising Code, the ISAF Eligibility Code and the ISAF Anti-Doping Code, which replace former Appendices G, K and L. These codes are ISAF regulations and are also racing rules. For more information see the preamble to Appendices, Section II.

Terminology A term used in the sense stated in the Definitions is printed in italics or, in preambles, in bold italics (for example, *racing* and **racing**). Other words and terms are used in the sense ordinarily understood in nautical or general use. 'Race committee' includes any person or committee performing a race committee function. 'Class rules' includes rules of handicapping and rating systems.

Appendices When the rules of an appendix apply, they take precedence over any conflicting rules in Parts 1–7. Each appendix is identified by a letter or a number. A reference to a rule in a lettered appendix will contain the letter of the appendix and the rule number (for example, 'rule A1'). There is no Appendix I. A reference to Appendix 1, 2 or 3 will contain the number of the appendix and the regulation number; for example, 'Appendix 1, Regulation 20.1'.

Changes to the Rules The prescriptions of a national authority, class rules or the sailing instructions may change a racing rule only as permitted by rule 86.

BASIC PRINCIPLE

SPORTSMANSHIP AND THE RULES

Competitors in the sport of sailing are governed by a body of *rules* that they are expected to follow and enforce. A fundamental principle of sportsmanship is that when competitors break a *rule* they will promptly take a penalty or retire.

PART 1 – FUNDAMENTAL RULES

1 SAFETY
1.1 Helping Those in Danger
A boat or competitor shall give all possible help to any person or vessel in danger.

1.2 Life-Saving Equipment and Personal Buoyancy
A boat shall carry adequate life-saving equipment for all persons on board, including one item ready for immediate use, unless her class rules make some other provision. Each competitor is individually responsible for wearing personal buoyancy adequate for the conditions.

2 FAIR SAILING
A boat and her owner shall compete in compliance with recognized principles of sportsmanship and fair play. A boat may be penalized under this rule only if it is clearly established that these principles have been violated. A disqualification under this rule shall not be excluded from the boat's series score.

3 ACCEPTANCE OF THE RULES
By participating in a race conducted under these racing rules,

each competitor and boat owner agrees

(a) to be governed by the *rules*;

(b) to accept the penalties imposed and other action taken under the *rules*, subject to the appeal and review procedures provided in them, as the final determination of any matter arising under the *rules*; and

(c) with respect to such determination, not to resort to any court or other tribunal not provided by the *rules*.

4 DECISION TO RACE
The responsibility for a boat's decision to participate in a race or to continue *racing* is hers alone.

5 DRUGS
A competitor shall neither take a substance nor use a method banned by the Olympic Movement Anti-Doping Code or the World Anti-Doping Agency and shall comply with Appendix 3 (ISAF Regulation 19, ISAF Anti-Doping Code). An alleged or actual breach of this rule shall be dealt with under Regulation 19. It shall not be grounds for a *protest* and rule 63.1 does not apply.

PART 2 – WHEN BOATS MEET

The rules of Part 2 apply between boats that are sailing in or near the racing area and intend to **race**, *are* **racing**, *or have been* **racing**. *However, a boat not* **racing** *shall not be penalized for breaking one of these rules, except rule 22.1. The International Regulations for Preventing Collisions at Sea or government right-of-way rules apply between a boat sailing under these rules and a vessel that is not, and they replace these rules if the sailing instructions so state.*

Section A – Right of Way

A boat has right of way when another boat is required to **keep clear** *of her. However, some rules in Sections B, C and D limit the actions of a right-of-way boat.*

10 ON OPPOSITE TACKS
When boats are on opposite tacks, a *port-tack* boat shall *keep clear* of a *starboard-tack* boat.

11 ON THE SAME TACK, OVERLAPPED
When boats are on the same *tack* and *overlapped*, a *windward* boat shall *keep clear* of a *leeward* boat.

12 ON THE SAME TACK, NOT OVERLAPPED
When boats are on the same *tack* and not *overlapped*, a boat *clear astern* shall *keep clear* of a boat *clear ahead*.

13 WHILE TACKING
After a boat passes head to wind, she shall *keep clear* of other boats until she is on a close-hauled course. During that time rules 10, 11 and 12 do not apply. If two boats are subject to this rule at the same time, the one on the other's port side shall *keep clear*.

Section B – General Limitations

14 AVOIDING CONTACT
A boat shall avoid contact with another boat if reasonably possible. However, a right-of-way boat or one entitled to *room*

(a) need not act to avoid contact until it is clear that the other boat is not *keeping clear* or giving *room*, and

(b) shall not be penalized under this rule unless there is contact that causes damage.

15 ACQUIRING RIGHT OF WAY
When a boat acquires right of way, she shall initially give the other boat *room* to *keep clear*, unless she acquires right of way because of the other boat's actions.

16 CHANGING COURSE

16.1 When a right-of-way boat changes course, she shall give the other boat room to *keep clear*.

16.2 In addition, when after the starting signal boats are about to cross or are crossing each other on opposite *tacks*, and the *port-tack* boat is *keeping clear* of the *starboard-tack* boat, the *starboard-tack* boat shall not change course if as a result the *port-tack* boat would immediately need to change course to continue *keeping clear*.

17 ON THE SAME TACK; PROPER COURSE

17.1 If a boat clear *astern* becomes *overlapped* within two of her hull lengths to *leeward* of a boat on the same *tack*, she shall not sail above her *proper course* while they remain *overlapped* within that distance, unless in doing so she promptly sails astern of the other boat. This rule does not apply if the *overlap* begins while the *windward* boat is required by rule 13 to *keep clear*.

17.2 Except on a beat to windward, while a boat is less than two of her hull lengths from a *leeward* boat or a boat *clear astern* steering a course to *leeward* of her, she shall not sail below her *proper course* unless she gybes.

Section C – At Marks and Obstructions

To the extent that a Section C rule conflicts with a rule in Section A or B, the Section C rule takes precedence.

18 ROUNDING AND PASSING MARKS AND OBSTRUCTIONS

*In rule 18, **room** is **room** for an inside boat to round or pass between an outside boat and a **mark** or **obstruction**, including **room** to tack or gybe when either is a normal part of the manoeuvre.*

18.1 When This Rule Applies

Rule 18 applies when boats are about to round or pass a *mark* they are required to leave on the same side, or an *obstruction* on the same side, until they have passed it. However, it does not apply

(a) at a starting *mark* surrounded by navigable water or at its anchor line from the time the boats are approaching them to *start* until they have passed them, or

(b) between boats on opposite *tacks*, either on a beat to windward or when the *proper course* for one or both of them to round or pass the mark or obstruction is to tack.

18.2 Giving Room; Keeping Clear

(a) OVERLAPPED – BASIC RULE

When boats are *overlapped* the outside boat shall give the inside boat *room* to round or pass the *mark* or *obstruction*, and if the inside boat has right of way the outside boat shall also *keep clear*. Other parts of rule 18 contain exceptions to this rule.

(b) OVERLAPPED AT THE ZONE

If boats were *overlapped* before either of them reached the *two-length zone* and the *overlap* is broken after one of them has reached it, the boat that was on the outside shall continue to give the other boat *room*. If the outside boat becomes *clear astern* or *overlapped* inside the other boat, she is not entitled to *room* and shall *keep clear*.

(c) NOT OVERLAPPED AT THE ZONE

If a boat is *clear ahead* at the time she reaches the *two-length zone*, the boat *clear astern* shall thereafter *keep clear*. If the boat *clear astern* becomes *overlapped* outside the other boat she shall also give the inside boat *room*. If the boat *clear astern* becomes *overlapped* inside the other boat she is not entitled to *room*. If the boat that was *clear ahead* passes head to wind, rule 18.2(c) no longer applies.

(d) CHANGING COURSE TO ROUND OR PASS

When rule 18 applies between two boats and the right-of-way boat is changing course to round or pass a *mark*, rule 16 does not apply between her and the other boat.

(e) OVERLAP RIGHTS

If there is reasonable doubt that a boat obtained or broke an *overlap* in time, it shall be presumed that she did not. If the outside boat is unable to give *room* when an *overlap* begins, rules 18.2(a) and 18.2(b) do not apply.

18.3 Tacking at a Mark

If two boats were approaching a *mark* on opposite *tacks* and one of them completes a tack in the *two-length zone* when the other is fetching the *mark*, rule 18.2 does not apply. The boat that tacked

(a) shall not cause the other boat to sail above close-hauled to avoid her or prevent the other boat from passing the *mark*, and

(b) shall give *room* if the other boat becomes *overlapped* inside her, in which case rule 15 does not apply.

18.4 Gybing

When an inside *overlapped* right-of-way boat must gybe at a *mark* or *obstruction* to sail her *proper course*, until she gybes she shall sail no farther from the *mark* or *obstruction* than needed to sail that course.

18.5 Passing a Continuing Obstruction

While boats are passing a continuing *obstruction*, rules 18.2(b) and 18.2(c) do not apply. A boat *clear astern* that obtains an inside *overlap* is entitled to *room* to pass between the other boat and the *obstruction* only if at the moment the *overlap* begins there is *room* to do so. If there is not, she is not entitled to *room* and shall *keep clear*.

19 ROOM TO TACK AT AN OBSTRUCTION

19.1 When safety requires a close-hauled boat to make a substantial course change to avoid an *obstruction* and she intends to *tack*, but cannot *tack* and avoid another boat on the same *tack*, she shall hail for *room* to do so. Before *tacking* she shall give the hailed boat time to respond. The hailed boat shall either

(a) tack as soon as possible, in which case the hailing boat shall also tack as soon as possible, or

(b) immediately reply 'You tack', in which case the hailing boat shall *tack* as soon as possible and the hailed boat shall give *room*, and rules 10 and 13 do not apply.

19.2 Rule 19.1 does not apply at a starting *mark* surrounded by navigable water or at its anchor line from the time boats are approaching them to start until they have passed them or at a *mark* that the hailed boat can fetch. When rule 19.1 applies, rule 18 does not.

Section D – Other Rules

When rule 20 or 21 applies between two boats, Section A rules do not.

20 STARTING ERRORS; PENALTY TURNS; MOVING ASTERN

A boat sailing towards the pre-start side of the starting line or its extensions after her starting signal to comply with rule 29.1 or 30.1 shall *keep clear* of a boat not doing so until she is completely on the pre-start side. A boat making a penalty turn shall *keep clear* of one that is not. A boat moving astern by backing a sail shall *keep clear* of one that is not.

21 CAPSIZED, ANCHORED OR AGROUND; RESCUING

If possible, a boat shall avoid a boat that is capsized or has not regained control after capsizing, is anchored or aground, or is trying to help a person or vessel in danger. A boat is capsized when her masthead is in the water.

22 INTERFERING WITH ANOTHER BOAT

22.1 If reasonably possible, a boat not *racing* shall not interfere with a boat that is *racing*.

22.2 A boat shall not deliberately interfere with a boat making penalty turns to delay her.

PART 3 – CONDUCT OF A RACE

25 SAILING INSTRUCTIONS AND SIGNALS

Sailing instructions shall be made available to each boat before a race begins. The meanings of the visual and sound signals stated in Race Signals shall not be changed except under rule 86.1(b). The meanings of any other signals that may be used shall be stated in the sailing instructions.

26 STARTING RACES

Races shall be started by using the following signals. Times shall be taken from the visual signals; the absence of a sound signal shall be disregarded.

Signal	Flag and sound	Minutes before starting signal
Warning	Class flag; 1 sound	5*
Preparatory	P, I, Z, Z with I, or black flag; 1 sound	4
One-minute	Preparatory flag removed; 1 long sound	1
Starting	Class flag removed; 1 sound	0

* or as stated in the sailing instructions
The warning signal for each succeeding class shall be made with or after the starting signal of the preceding class.

27 OTHER RACE COMMITTEE ACTIONS BEFORE THE STARTING SIGNAL

27.1 No later than the warning signal, the race committee shall signal or otherwise designate the course to be sailed if the sailing instructions have not stated the course, and it may replace one course signal with another, signal that a designated short course will be used (display flag S with two sounds), and signal that wearing personal buoyancy is required (display flag Y with one sound).

27.2 No later than the preparatory signal, the race committee may move a starting *mark* and may apply rule 30.

27.3 Before the starting signal, the race committee may for any reason *postpone* (display flag AP, AP over H, or AP over A, with two sounds) or abandon the race (display flag N over H, or N over A, with three sounds).

28 SAILING THE COURSE

28.1 A boat shall *start*, leave each *mark* on the required side in the correct order, and *finish*, so that a string representing her wake after *starting* and until *finishing* would when drawn taut pass each *mark* on the required side and touch each rounding *mark*. After *finishing* she need not cross the *finishing* line completely. She may correct any errors to comply with this rule, provided she has not already finished.

28.2 A boat may leave on either side a *mark* that does not begin, bound or end the leg she is on. However, she shall leave a starting *mark* on the required side when she is approaching the starting line from its pre-start side to *start*.

29 STARTING; RECALLS

29.1 On the Course Side at the Start

When at a boat's starting signal any part of her hull, crew or equipment is on the course side of the starting line, she shall sail completely to the pre-start side of the line before *starting*.

29.2 Individual Recall

When at a boat's starting signal she must comply with rule 29.1 or 30.1, the race committee shall promptly display flag X with one sound. The flag shall be displayed until all such boats are completely on the pre-start side of the starting line or its extensions and have complied with rule 30.1 if it applies, but not later than four minutes after the starting signal or one minute before any later starting signal, whichever is earlier.

29.3 General Recall

When at the starting signal the race committee is unable to identify boats that are on the course side of the starting line or to which rule 30 applies, or there has been an error in the starting procedure, the race committee may signal a general recall (display the First Substitute with two sounds). The warning signal for a new start for the recalled class shall be made one minute after the First Substitute is removed (one sound), and the starts for any succeeding classes shall follow the new start.

30 STARTING PENALTIES

30.1 Round-an-End Rule

If flag I has been displayed before, with, or as a boat's preparatory signal, and any part of her hull, crew or equipment is on the course side of the starting line or its extensions during the minute before her starting signal, she shall sail to the pre-start side of the line around either end before *starting*.

30.2 20% Penalty Rule

If flag Z has been displayed before, with, or as a boat's preparatory signal, she shall not enter the triangle formed by the ends of the starting line and the first *mark* with any part of her hull, crew or equipment during the minute before her starting signal. If she is identified as having done so, she shall receive, without a hearing, a 20% scoring penalty calculated as stated in rule 44.3(c). She shall be penalized even if the race is restarted, resailed or rescheduled, but not if it is *postponed* or *abandoned* before the starting signal.

30.3 Black Flag Rule

If a black flag has been displayed before, with, or as a boat's preparatory signal, she shall not enter the triangle formed by the ends of the starting line and the first *mark* with any part of her hull, crew or equipment during the minute before her starting signal. If she is identified as having done so, she shall be disqualified without a hearing, even if the race is restarted, resailed or rescheduled, but not if it is *postponed* or *abandoned* after the starting signal. If a general recall is signalled or the race is *abandoned* after the starting signal, the race committee shall display her sail number, and if the race is restarted or resailed she shall not sail in it. If she does so, her disqualification shall not be excluded in calculating her series score.

31 TOUCHING A MARK

31.1 While *racing*, a boat shall not touch a *starting mark* before *starting*, a *mark* that begins, bounds or ends the leg of the course on which she is sailing, or a finishing *mark* after *finishing*.

31.2 A boat that has broken rule 31.1 may, after getting well clear of other boats as soon as possible, take a penalty by promptly making one complete 360° turn including one *tack* and one gybe. When a boat takes the penalty after touching a finishing *mark*, she shall sail completely to the course side of the line before *finishing*. However, if a boat has gained a significant advantage in the race or series by touching the *mark* she shall retire.

32 SHORTENING OR ABANDONING AFTER THE START

32.1 After the starting signal, the race committee may *abandon* the race (display flag N, N over H, or N over A, with three sounds) or shorten the course (display flag S with two sounds), as appropriate,

(a) because of an error in the starting procedure,

(b) because of foul weather,

(c) because of insufficient wind making it unlikely that any boat will *finish* within the time limit,

(d) because a *mark* is missing or out of position, or

(e) for any other reason directly affecting the safety or fairness of the competition.

However, after one boat has sailed the course and *finished* within the time limit, if any, the race committee shall not *abandon* the race without considering the consequences for all boats in the race or series.

32.2 After the starting signal, the race committee may shorten the course (display flag S with two sounds) to enable further scheduled races to be sailed.

33 CHANGING THE POSITION OF THE NEXT MARK

At any rounding *mark* the race committee may signal a change of the direction of the next leg of the course by displaying flag C with repetitive sounds and the compass bearing of that leg before any boat begins it. The race committee may change the length of the next leg by displaying flag C with repetitive sounds and a '–' if the leg will be shortened or a '+' if the leg will be lengthened.

34 MARK MISSING

When a *mark* is missing or out of position, the race committee shall, if possible,

(a) replace it in its correct position or

(b) substitute one of similar appearance, or a buoy or vessel displaying flag M with repetitive sounds.

35 TIME LIMIT AND SCORES

If one boat sails the course as required by rule 28.1 and *finishes* within the time limit, if any, all boats that *finish* shall be scored according to their *finishing* places unless the race is *abandoned*. If no boat finishes within the time limit, the race committee shall *abandon* the race.

36 RACES TO BE RESTARTED OR RESAILED

If a race is restarted or resailed, a breach of a *rule*, other than rule 30.3, in the original race shall not prohibit a boat from competing or, except under rule 30.2, 30.3 or 69, cause her to be penalized.

PART 4 – OTHER REQUIREMENTS WHEN RACING

*Part 4 rules apply only to boats **racing**.*

40 PERSONAL BUOYANCY

When flag Y is displayed with one sound before or with the warning signal, competitors shall wear life-jackets or other adequate personal buoyancy. Wet suits and dry suits are not adequate personal buoyancy.

41 OUTSIDE HELP

A boat may receive outside help as provided for in rule 1. Otherwise, she shall not receive help except for an ill or injured crew member or, after a collision, from the crew of the other boat.

42 PROPULSION

42.1 Basic Rule

Except when permitted in rule 42.3 or 45, a boat shall compete by using only the wind and water to increase, maintain or decrease her speed. Her crew may adjust the trim of sails and hull, and perform other acts of seamanship, but shall not otherwise move their bodies to propel the boat.

42.2 Prohibited Actions

Without limiting the application of rule 42.1, these actions are prohibited:

(a) pumping: repeated fanning of any sail either by trimming and releasing the sail or by vertical or athwartships body movement;

(b) rocking: repeated rolling of the boat, induced either by body movement or adjustment of the sails or centreboard, that does not facilitate steering;

(c) ooching: sudden forward body movement, stopped abruptly;

(d) sculling: repeated movement of the helm not necessary for steering;

(e) repeated tacks or gybes unrelated to changes in the wind or to tactical considerations.

42.3 Exceptions

(a) A boat's crew may move their bodies to exaggerate the rolling that facilitates steering the boat through a tack or a gybe, provided that, just after the tack or gybe is completed, the boat's speed is not greater than it would have been in the absence of the tack or gybe.

(b) Except on a beat to windward, when surfing (rapidly accelerating down the leeward side of a wave) or planing is possible, the boat's crew may pull the sheet and the guy controlling any sail in order to initiate surfing or planing, but only once for each wave or gust of wind.

(c) Any means of propulsion may be used to help a person or another vessel in danger.

(d) To get clear after grounding or colliding with another boat or object, a boat may use force applied by the crew of either boat and any equipment other than a propulsion engine.

43 COMPETITOR CLOTHING AND EQUIPMENT

43.1 (a) Competitors shall not wear or carry clothing or equipment for the purpose of increasing their weight.

(b) Furthermore, a competitor's clothing and equipment shall not weigh more than 8 kilograms, excluding a hiking or trapeze harness and clothing (including footwear) worn only below the knee. Class rules or sailing instructions may specify a lower weight or a higher weight up to 10 kilograms. Class rules may include footwear and other clothing worn below the knee within that weight. A hiking or trapeze harness shall have positive buoyancy and shall not weigh more than 2 kilograms, except that class rules may specify a higher weight up to 4 kilograms. Weights shall be determined as required by Appendix H.

(c) When a measurer in charge of weighing clothing and equipment believes a competitor may have broken rule 43.1(a) or 43.1(b) he shall report the matter in writing to the race committee, which shall protest the boat of the competitor.

43.2 Rule 43.1(b) does not apply to boats required to be equipped with lifelines.

44 PENALTIES FOR BREAKING RULES OF PART 2

44.1 Taking a Penalty

A boat that may have broken a rule of Part 2 while *racing* may take a penalty at the time of the incident. Her penalty shall be a 720° Turns Penalty unless the sailing instructions specify the use of the Scoring Penalty or some other penalty. However, if she caused serious damage or gained a significant advantage in the race or series by her breach she shall retire.

44.2 720° Turns Penalty

After getting well clear of other boats as soon after the incident as possible, a boat takes a 720° Turns Penalty by promptly making two complete 360° turns (720°) in the same direction, including two tacks and two gybes. When a boat takes the penalty at or near the finishing line, she shall sail completely to the course side of the line before *finishing*.

44.3 Scoring Penalty

(a) A boat takes a Scoring Penalty by displaying a yellow flag at the first reasonable opportunity after the incident, keeping it displayed until finishing, and calling the race committee's attention to it at the finishing line. At that time she shall also inform the race committee of the identity of the other boat involved in the incident. If this is impracticable, she shall do so at the first reasonable opportunity within the time limit for protests.

(b) If a boat displays a yellow flag, she shall also comply with the other parts of rule 44.3(a).

(c) The boat's penalty score shall be the score for the place worse than her actual finishing place by the number of places stated in the sailing instructions, except that she shall not be scored worse than Did Not Finish. When the sailing instructions do not state the number of places, the number shall be the whole number (rounding 0.5 upward) nearest to 20% of the number of boats entered. The scores of other boats shall not be changed; therefore, two boats may receive the same score.

44.4 Limits on Penalties

(a) When a boat intends to take a penalty as provided in rule 44.1 and in the same incident has touched a *mark*, she need not take the penalty provided in rule 31.2.

(b) A boat that takes a penalty shall not be penalized further with respect to the same incident unless she failed to retire when rule 44.1 required her to do so.

45 HAULING OUT; MAKING FAST; ANCHORING

A boat shall be afloat and off moorings at her preparatory signal. Thereafter, she shall not be hauled out or made fast except to bail out, reef sails or make repairs. She may anchor or the crew may stand on the bottom. She shall recover the anchor before continuing in the race unless she is unable to do so.

46 PERSON IN CHARGE

A boat shall have on board a person in charge designated by the member or organization that entered the boat. See rule 75.

47 LIMITATIONS ON EQUIPMENT AND CREW

47.1 A boat shall use only the equipment on board at her preparatory signal.

47.2 No person on board shall intentionally leave, except when ill or injured, or to help a person or vessel in danger, or to swim. A person leaving the boat by accident or to swim shall be back on board before the boat continues in the race.

48 FOG SIGNALS AND LIGHTS

When safety requires, a boat shall sound fog signals and show lights as required by the *International Regulations for Preventing Collisions at Sea* or applicable government rules.

49 CREW POSITION

49.1 Competitors shall use no device designed to position their bodies outboard, other than hiking straps and stiffeners worn under the thighs.

49.2 When lifelines are required by the class rules or the sailing instructions they shall be taut, and competitors shall not position any part of their torsos outside them, except briefly to perform a necessary task. On boats equipped with upper and lower lifelines of wire, a competitor sitting on the deck facing outboard with his waist inside the lower lifeline may have the upper part of his body outside the upper lifeline.

50 SETTING AND SHEETING SAILS

50.1 Changing Sails

When headsails or spinnakers are being changed, a replacing sail may be fully set and trimmed before the replaced sail is lowered. However, only one mainsail and, except when changing, only one spinnaker shall be carried set at a time.

50.2 Spinnaker Poles, Whisker Poles
Only one spinnaker pole or whisker pole shall be used at a time except when gybing. When in use, it shall be attached to the foremost mast.

50.3 Use of Outriggers
(a) No sail shall be sheeted over or through an outrigger, except as permitted in rule 50.3(b). An outrigger is any fitting or other device so placed that it could exert outward pressure on a sheet or sail at a point from which, with the boat upright, a vertical line would fall outside the hull or deck planking. For the purpose of this rule, bulwarks, rails and rubbing strakes are not part of the hull or deck planking and the following are not outriggers: a bowsprit used to secure the tack of a working sail, a bumkin used to sheet the boom of a working sail, or a boom of a boomed headsail that requires no adjustment when tacking.

(b) (1) Any sail may be sheeted to or led above a boom that is regularly used for a working sail and is permanently attached to the mast from which the head of the working sail is set.

(2) A headsail may be sheeted or attached at its clew to a spinnaker pole or whisker pole, provided that a spinnaker is not set.

50.4 Headsails
The difference between a headsail and a spinnaker is that the mid-girth of a headsail, measured from the mid-points of its luff and leech, does not exceed 50% of the length of its foot, and no other intermediate girth exceeds a percentage similarly proportional to its distance from the head of the sail. A sail tacked down behind the foremost mast is not a headsail.

51 MOVABLE BALLAST
All movable ballast shall be properly stowed, and water, dead weight or ballast shall not be moved for the purpose of changing trim or stability. Floorboards, bulkheads, doors, stairs and water tanks shall be left in place and all cabin fixtures kept on board.

52 MANUAL POWER
A boat's standing rigging, running rigging, spars and movable hull appendages shall be adjusted and operated only by manual power.

53 SKIN FRICTION
A boat shall not eject or release a substance, such as a polymer, or have specially textured surfaces that could improve the character of the flow of water inside the boundary layer.

54 FORESTAYS AND HEADSAIL TACKS
Forestays and headsail tacks, except those of spinnaker staysails when the boat is not close-hauled, shall be attached approximately on a boat's centre-line.

PART 5 – PROTESTS, REDRESS, HEARINGS, MISCONDUCT AND APPEALS

Section A – Protests and Redress

60 RIGHT TO PROTEST AND REQUEST REDRESS
60.1 A boat may

(a) protest another boat, but not for an alleged breach of a rule of Part 2 unless she was involved in or saw the incident; or

(b) request redress.

60.2 A race committee may
(a) protest a boat, but not as a result of a report by a competitor from another boat or other *interested party* or of information in an invalid protest;

(b) request redress for a boat; or

(c) report to the protest committee requesting action under rule 69.1(a).

60.3 A protest committee may
(a) protest a boat, but not as a result of a report by a competitor from another boat or other *interested party* except under rule 61.1(c), or as a result of information in an invalid *protest* except under rule 60.4;

(b) call a hearing to consider redress; or

(c) act under rule 69.1(a).

60.4 If a protest committee receives a report of an incident that may

have resulted in serious damage or serious injury, it may protest any boat involved.

61 PROTEST REQUIREMENTS
61.1 Informing the Protestee
(a) A boat intending to protest shall always inform the other boat at the first reasonable opportunity. When her *protest* concerns an incident in the racing area that she is involved in or sees, she shall hail 'Protest' and conspicuously display a red flag at the first reasonable opportunity for each. However, boats of hull length less than 6 metres need not display the flag, and if the other boat is beyond hailing distance the protesting boat need not hail but shall inform the other boat at the first reasonable opportunity. A boat required to display a flag shall do so until she is no longer *racing*.

(b) A race committee or protest committee intending to protest a boat under rule 60.2(a) or 60.3(a) shall inform her as soon as reasonably possible, except that if the *protest* arises from an incident it observes in the racing area the committee shall inform the boat after the race within the time limit of rule 61.3.

(c) During the hearing of a valid *protest* or request for redress, if the protest committee decides to protest a boat that was involved in the incident but is not a *party* to that hearing, it shall inform the boat as soon as reasonably possible of its intention, then protest her as required by rule 61.2 and proceed with a hearing as required by rule 63.

61.2 Protest Contents
A *protest* shall be in writing and identify

(a) the protestor and protestee;

(b) the incident, including where and when it occurred;

(c) any *rule* the protestor believes was broken; and

(d) the name of the protestor's representative.

Provided the written *protest* identifies the incident, other details may be corrected before or during the hearing.

61.3 Protest Time Limit
A *protest* by a boat, or by the race committee or protest committee about an incident the committee observes in the racing area, shall be delivered to the race office no later than the time limit stated in the sailing instructions. If none is stated, the time limit is two hours after the last boat in the race *finishes*. Other race committee or protest committee *protests* shall be delivered to the race office within two hours after the committee receives the relevant information. The protest committee shall extend the time if there is good reason to do so.

62 REDRESS
62.1 A request for redress or a protest committee's decision to consider redress shall be based on a claim or possibility that a boat's finishing place in a race or series has, through no fault of her own, been made significantly worse by

(a) an improper action or omission of the race committee or protest committee,

(b) physical damage because of the action of a boat that was breaking a rule of Part 2 or of a vessel not *racing* that was required to *keep clear*,

(c) giving help (except to herself or her crew) in compliance with rule 1.1, or

(d) a boat against which a penalty has been imposed under rule 2 or disciplinary action has been taken under rule 69.1(b).

62.2 The request shall be made in writing within the time limit of rule 61.3 or within two hours of the relevant incident, whichever is later. The protest committee shall extend the time if there is good reason to do so. No red flag is required.

Section B – Hearings and Decisions

63 HEARINGS
63.1 Requirement for a Hearing
A boat or competitor shall not be penalized without a protest hearing, except as provided in rules 30.2, 30.3, 67, 69, A5 and N2. A decision on redress shall not be made without a hearing. The protest committee shall hear all *protests* and requests for redress that have been delivered to the race office unless it allows a boat to withdraw her *protest* or request.

63.2 Time and Place of the Hearing; Time for Parties to Prepare
All *parties* to the hearing shall be notified of the time and place of the hearing, the *protest* or redress information shall be made available to them, and they shall be allowed reasonable time to prepare for the hearing.

63.3 m Right to Be Present
(a) The *parties* to the hearing, or a representative of each, have the right to be present throughout the hearing of all the evidence. When a *protest* claims a breach of a rule of Part 2, 3 or 4, the representatives of boats shall have been on board at the time of the incident, unless there is good reason for the protest committee to rule otherwise. Any witness, other than a member of the protest committee, shall be excluded except when giving evidence.

(b) If a *party* to the hearing does not come to the hearing, the protest committee may nevertheless decide the *protest* or request for redress. If the *party* was unavoidably absent, the committee may reopen the hearing.

63.4 Interested Party
A member of a protest committee who is an *interested party* shall not take any further part in the hearing but may appear as a witness. A party to the hearing who believes a member of the protest committee is an *interested party* shall object as soon as possible.

63.5 Validity of the Protest or Request for Redress
At the beginning of the hearing the protest committee shall decide whether all requirements for the *protest* or request for redress have been met, after first taking any evidence it considers necessary. If all requirements have been met, the *protest* or request is valid and the hearing shall be continued. If not, it shall be closed. If the *protest* has been made under rule 60.4, the protest committee must also determine whether or not serious damage or serious injury resulted from the incident in question. If not, the hearing shall be closed.

63.6 Taking Evidence and Finding Facts
The protest committee shall take the evidence of the *parties* to the hearing and of their witnesses and other evidence it considers necessary. A member of the protest committee who saw the incident may give evidence. A *party* to the hearing may question any person who gives evidence. The committee shall then find the facts and base its decision on them.

63.7 Protests Between Boats in Different Races
A *protest* between boats sailing in different races conducted by different organizing authorities shall be heard by a protest committee acceptable to those authorities.

64 DECISIONS
64.1 Penalties and Exoneration
(a) When the protest committee decides that a boat that is a *party* to a protest hearing has broken a *rule*, it shall disqualify her unless some other penalty applies. A penalty shall be imposed whether or not the applicable rule was mentioned in the *protest*.

(b) When as a consequence of breaking a *rule* a boat has compelled another boat to break a *rule*, rule 64.1(a) does not apply to the other boat and she shall be exonerated.

(c) If a boat has broken a *rule* when not *racing*, her penalty shall apply to the race sailed nearest in time to that of the incident.

64.2 Decisions on Redress
When the protest committee decides that a boat is entitled to redress under rule 62, it shall make as fair an arrangement as possible for all boats affected, whether or not they asked for redress. This may be to adjust the scoring (see rule A10 for some examples) or finishing times of boats, to *abandon* the race, to let the results stand or to make some other arrangement. When in doubt about the facts or probable results of any arrangement for the race or series, especially before *abandon*ing the race, the protest committee shall take evidence from appropriate sources.

64.3 Decisions on Measurement Protests
(a) When the protest committee finds that deviations in excess of tolerances specified in the class rules were caused by damage or normal wear and do not improve the performance of the boat, it shall not penalize her. However, the boat shall not *race* again until the deviations have been corrected, except when the protest committee decides there is or has been no reasonable opportunity to do so.

(b) When the protest committee is in doubt about the meaning of a measurement rule, it shall refer its questions, together with the relevant facts, to an authority responsible for interpreting the rule. In making its decision, the committee shall be bound by the reply of the authority.

(c) When a boat disqualified under a measurement rule states in writing that she intends to appeal, she may compete in subsequent races without changes to the boat, but will be disqualified if she fails to appeal or the appeal is decided against her.

(d) Measurement costs arising from a *protest* involving a measurement rule shall be paid by the unsuccessful *party* unless the protest committee decides otherwise.

65 INFORMING THE PARTIES AND OTHERS
65.1 After making its decision, the protest committee shall promptly inform the *parties* to the hearing of the facts found, the applicable *rules*, the decision, the reasons for it, and any penalties imposed or redress given.

65.2 A *party* to the hearing is entitled to receive the above information in writing, provided she asks for it in writing from the protest committee within seven days of being informed of the decision. The committee shall then promptly provide the information, including, when relevant, a diagram of the incident prepared or endorsed by the committee.

65.3 When the protest committee penalizes a boat under a measurement rule, it shall send the above information to the relevant measurement authorities.

66 REOPENING A HEARING
The protest committee may reopen a hearing when it decides that it may have made a significant error, or when significant new evidence becomes available within a reasonable time. It shall reopen a hearing when required by the national authority under rule F5. A *party* to the hearing may ask for a reopening no later than 24 hours after being informed of the decision. When a hearing is reopened, a majority of the members of the protest committee shall, if possible, be members of the original protest committee.

67 RULE 42 AND HEARING REQUIREMENT
When so stated in the sailing instructions, the protest committee may penalize without a hearing a boat that has broken rule 42, provided that a member of the committee or its designated observer has seen the incident, and a disqualification under this rule shall not be excluded from the boat's series score. A boat so penalized shall be informed by notification in the race results.

68 DAMAGES
The question of damages arising from a breach of any *rule* shall be governed by the prescriptions, if any, of the national authority.

Section C – Gross Misconduct

69 ALLEGATIONS OF GROSS MISCONDUCT
69.1 Action by a Protest Committee
(a) When a protest committee, from its own observation or a report received, believes that a competitor may have committed a gross breach of a *rule* or of good manners or sportsmanship, or may have brought the sport into disrepute, it may call a hearing. The protest committee shall promptly inform the competitor in writing of the alleged misconduct and of the time and place of the hearing.

(b) A protest committee of at least three members shall conduct the hearing, following rules 63.2, 63.3, 63.4 and 63.6. If it decides that the competitor committed the alleged misconduct it shall either

(1) warn the competitor or

(2) impose a penalty by excluding the competitor, and a boat when appropriate, from a race, or the remaining races of a series or the entire series, or by taking other action within its jurisdiction.

(c) The protest committee shall promptly report a penalty, but not a warning, to the national authorities of the venue, of the competitor and of the boat owner.

(d) If the competitor has left the venue and cannot be notified or fails to attend the hearing, the protest committee shall collect all available evidence and, when the allegation seems justified, make a report to the relevant national authorities.

(e) When the protest committee has left the event and a report alleging misconduct is received, the race committee or organizing authority may appoint a new protest committee to proceed under this rule.

69.2 Action by a National Authority

(a) When a national authority receives a report required by rule 69.1(c) or 69.1(d), or a report alleging a gross breach of a *rule* or of good manners or sportsmanship or conduct that brought the sport into disrepute, it may conduct an investigation and, when appropriate, shall conduct a hearing. It may then take any disciplinary action within its jurisdiction it considers appropriate against the competitor or boat, or other person involved, including suspending eligibility, permanently or for a specified period of time, to compete in any event held within its jurisdiction, and suspending ISAF eligibility under Appendix 2, Regulation 21.3.1(a).

(b) The national authority of a competitor shall also suspend the ISAF eligibility of the competitor as required in Appendix 2, Regulation 21.3.1(a).

(c) The national authority shall promptly report a suspension of eligibility under rule 69.2(a) to the ISAF, and to the national authorities of the person or the owner of the boat suspended if they are not members of the suspending national authority.

69.3 Action by the ISAF

Upon receipt of a report required by rules 69.2(c) and Appendix 2, Regulation 21.4.1, the ISAF shall inform all national authorities, which may also suspend eligibility for events held within their jurisdiction. The ISAF Executive Committee shall suspend the competitor's ISAF eligibility as required in Appendix 2, Regulation 21.3.1(a) if the competitor's national authority does not do so.

Section D – Appeals

70 RIGHT OF APPEAL AND REQUESTS FOR INTERPRETATION

70.1 Provided that the right of appeal has not been denied under rule 70.4, a protest committee's interpretation of a *rule* or its procedures, but not the facts in its decision, may be appealed to the national authority of the venue by

(a) a boat or competitor that is a *party* to a hearing, or

(b) a race committee that is a *party* to a hearing, provided the protest committee is a jury.

70.2 A protest committee may request confirmation or correction of its decision.

70.3 A club or other organization affiliated to a national authority may request an interpretation of the *rules*, provided that no *protest* or request for redress that may be appealed is involved.

70.4 There shall be no appeal from the decisions of an international jury constituted in compliance with Appendix M. Furthermore, if the notice of race and the sailing instructions so state, the right of appeal may be denied provided that

(a) it is essential to determine promptly the result of a race that will qualify a boat to compete in a later stage of an event or a subsequent event (a national authority may prescribe that its approval is required for such a procedure),

(b) a national authority so approves for a particular event open only to entrants under its own jurisdiction, or

(c) a national authority after consultation with the ISAF so approves for a particular event, provided the jury is constituted as required by Appendix M, except that only two members of the jury need be International Judges.

70.5 Appeals and requests shall conform to Appendix F.

71 APPEAL DECISIONS

71.1 No *interested party* or member of the *protest* committee shall take any part in the discussion or decision on an appeal or a request for confirmation or correction.

71.2 The national authority may uphold, change or reverse the protest committee's decision, declare the *protest* or request for redress invalid, or return the *protest* or request for a new hearing and decision by the same or a different protest committee.

71.3 When from the facts found by the protest committee the national authority decides that a boat that was a *party* to a *protest* hearing broke a *rule*, it shall penalize her, whether or not that boat or that *rule* was mentioned in the protest committee's decision.

71.4 The decision of the national authority shall be final. The national authority shall send its decision in writing to all *parties* to the hearing and the protest committee, who shall be bound by the decision.

PART 6 – ENTRY AND QUALIFICATION

75 ENTERING A RACE

75.1 To enter a race, a boat shall comply with the requirements of the organizing authority of the race. She shall be entered by

(a) a member of a club or other organization affiliated to a national authority,

(b) such a club or organization, or

(c) a member of a national authority.

75.2 Competitors shall comply with Appendix 2.

76 EXCLUSION OF BOATS OR COMPETITORS

76.1 The organizing authority or the race committee may reject or cancel the entry of a boat or exclude a competitor, subject to rule 76.2, provided it does so before the start of the first race and states the reason for doing so. However, the organizing authority or the race committee shall not reject or cancel the entry of a boat or exclude a competitor because of advertising, provided the boat or competitor complies with Appendix 1.

76.2 At world and continental championships no entry within stated quotas shall be rejected or cancelled without first obtaining the approval of the relevant international class association (or the Offshore Racing Council) or the ISAF.

77 IDENTIFICATION ON SAILS

A boat shall comply with the requirements of Appendix G governing class insignia, national letters and numbers on sails.

78 COMPLIANCE WITH CLASS RULES; CERTIFICATES

78.1 A boat's owner and any other person in charge shall ensure that the boat is maintained to comply with her class rules and that her measurement or rating certificate, if any, remains valid.

78.2 When a *rule* requires a certificate to be produced before a boat races, and it is not produced, the boat may *race* provided that the race committee receives a statement signed by the person in charge that a valid certificate exists and that it will be given to the race committee before the end of the event. If the certificate is not received in time, the boat's scores shall be removed from the event results.

78.3 When a measurer for an event concludes that a boat or personal equipment does not comply with the class rules, he shall report the matter in writing to the race committee, which shall protest the boat.

79 ADVERTISING

A boat and her crew shall comply with Appendix 1.

80 RESCHEDULED RACES

When a race has been rescheduled, rule 36 applies and all boats entered in the original race shall be notified and, unless disqualified under rule 30.3, be entitled to sail the rescheduled race. New entries that meet the entry requirements of the original race may be accepted at the discretion of the race committee.

PART 7 – RACE ORGANIZATION

85 GOVERNING RULES

The organizing authority, race committee and protest committee shall be governed by the rules in the conduct and judging of races.

86 RULE CHANGES

86.1 A racing rule may not be changed unless permitted in the rule itself or as follows:

(a) Prescriptions of a national authority may change a racing rule, but not the Definitions; a rule in the Introduction; Sportsmanship and the Rules; Part 1, 2 or 7; rule 43.1, 43.2, 69, 70, 71, 75, 76.2 or 79; a rule of an appendix that changes one of these rules; or Appendix H, M, 1, 2 or 3.

(b) Sailing instructions may change a racing rule by referring specifically to it and stating the change, but not rule 76.1, Appendix F, or a rule listed in rule 86.1(a).

(c) Class rules may change only racing rules 42, 49, 50, 51, 52, 53 and 54.

86.2 If a national authority so prescribes, these restrictions do not apply if rules are changed to develop or test proposed rules in local races. The national authority may prescribe that its approval is required for such changes.

87 ORGANIZING AUTHORITY; NOTICE OF RACE; APPOINTMENT OF RACE OFFICIALS

87.1 Organizing Authority
Races shall be organized by an organizing authority, which shall be

(a) the ISAF;

(b) a member national authority of the ISAF;

(c) a club or other organization affiliated to a national authority;

(d) a class association, either with the approval of a national authority or in conjunction with an affiliated club; or

(e) an unaffiliated body in conjunction with an affiliated club, except that in a major event designated by the ISAF, the unaffiliated body shall be owned and controlled by an affiliated club which shall have the approval of the relevant national authority.

87.2 Notice of Race; Appointment of Race Officials
The organizing authority shall publish a notice of race that conforms to rule J1, appoint a race committee and, when appropriate, appoint a jury. However, the race committee, an international jury and umpires may be appointed by the ISAF as provided by the ISAF regulations.

88 RACE COMMITTEE; SAILING INSTRUCTIONS; SCORING

88.1 Race Committee
The race committee shall conduct races as directed by the organizing authority and as required by the *rules*.

88.2 Sailing Instructions
(a) The race committee shall publish written sailing instructions that conform to rule J2.

(b) The sailing instructions for an international event shall include, in English, the applicable prescriptions of the national authority.

(c) Changes to the sailing instructions shall be in writing and posted within the required time on the official notice board or, on the water, communicated to each boat before her warning signal. Oral changes may be given only on the water, and only if the procedure is stated in the sailing instructions.

88.3 Scoring
(a) The race committee shall score a race or series as provided in Appendix A using either the Low Point or Bonus Point system, or as otherwise specified in the sailing instructions.

(b) When a scoring system provides for excluding one or more race scores from a boat's series score, the score for a breach of rule 2, rule 30.3's next-to-last sentence, or rule 42 if rule 67, N2.2 or N2.3 applies, shall not be excluded. The next-worse score shall be excluded instead.

89 PROTEST COMMITTEE
A protest committee shall be

(a) a committee appointed by the race committee;

(b) a jury appointed by the organizing authority, which is separate from and independent of the race committee; or

(c) an international jury appointed by the organizing authority or as prescribed in the ISAF regulations and meeting the requirements of Appendix M. A national authority may prescribe that its approval is required for the appointment of international juries for races within its jurisdiction, except ISAF events or when international juries are appointed by the ISAF under rule 87.2.

APPENDICES, SECTION I
APPENDIX A – SCORING

See rule 88.3.

A1 NUMBER OF RACES
The number of races scheduled and the number required to be completed to constitute a series shall be stated in the sailing instructions.

A2 SERIES SCORES
Each boat's series score shall be the total of her race scores excluding her worst score. (The sailing instructions may make a different arrangement by providing, for example, that no score will be excluded, that two or more scores will be excluded, or that a specified number of scores will be excluded if a specified number of races are completed.) If a boat has two or more equal worst scores, the score(s) for the race(s) sailed earliest in the series shall be excluded. The boat with the lowest series score wins and others shall be ranked accordingly.

A3 STARTING TIMES AND FINISHING PLACES
The time of a boat's starting signal shall be her starting time, and the order in which boats *finish* a race shall determine their finishing places. However, when a handicap system is used a boat's elapsed time, corrected to the nearest second, shall determine her finishing place.

A4 LOW POINT AND BONUS POINT SYSTEMS
Most series are scored using either the Low Point System or the Bonus Point System. The Low Point System uses a boat's finishing place as her race score. The Bonus Point System benefits the first six finishers because of the greater difficulty in advancing from fourth place to third, for example, than from fourteenth place to thirteenth. The system chosen may be made to apply by stating in the sailing instructions that, for example, 'The series will be scored as provided in Appendix A of the racing rules using the [Low] [Bonus] Point System.'

A4.1 Each boat *starting* and *finishing* and not thereafter retiring, being penalized or given redress shall be scored points as follows:

Finishing place	Low Point System	Bonus Point System
First	1	0
Second	2	3
Third	3	5.7
Fourth	4	8
Fifth	5	10
Sixth	6	11.7
Seventh	7	13
Each place thereafter	Add 1 point	Add 1 point

A4.2 A boat that did not *start*, did not *finish*, retired after *finishing* or was disqualified shall be scored points for the finishing place one more than the number of boats entered in the series. A boat penalized under rule 30.2 or 44.3 shall be scored points as provided in rule 44.3(c).

A5 SCORES DETERMINED BY THE RACE COMMITTEE
A boat that did not *start*, comply with rule 30.2 or 30.3, or *finish*, or that takes a penalty under rule 44.3 or retires after *finishing*, shall be scored accordingly by the race committee without a hearing. Only the protest committee may take other scoring actions that worsen a boat's score.

A6 CHANGES IN PLACES AND SCORES OF OTHER BOATS
(a) If a boat is disqualified from a race or retires after *finishing*, each boat that *finished* after her shall be moved up one place.

(b) If the protest committee decides to give redress by adjusting a boat's score, the scores of other boats shall not be changed unless the protest committee decides otherwise.

A7 RACE TIES
If boats are tied at the finishing line or if a handicap system is used and boats have equal corrected times, the points for the place for which the boats have tied and for the place(s) immediately below shall be added together and divided equally. Boats tied for a race prize shall share it or be given equal prizes.

A8 SERIES TIES
A8.1 If there is a series score tie between two or more boats, each boat's race scores shall be listed in order of best to worst, and at the first point(s) where there is a difference the tie shall be broken in favour of the boat(s) with the best score(s). No excluded scores shall be used.

A8.2 If a tie remains between two boats, it shall be broken in favour of the boat that scored better than the other boat in more races. If more than two boats are tied, they shall be ranked in order of the number of times each boat scored better than another of the tied boats. No race for which a tied boat's score has been excluded shall be used.

A8.3 If a tie still remains between two or more boats, they shall be ranked in order of their scores in the last race. Any remaining ties shall be broken by using the tied boats' scores in the next-to-last race and so on until all ties are broken. These scores shall be used even if some of them are excluded scores.

A9 RACE SCORES IN A SERIES LONGER THAN A REGATTA
For a series that is held over a period of time longer than a regatta, a boat that came to the starting area but did not *start*, did not *finish*, retired after *finishing* or was disqualified shall be scored points for the finishing place one more than the number of boats that came to the starting area. A boat that did not come to the starting area shall be scored points for the finishing place one more than the number of boats entered in the series.

A10 GUIDANCE ON REDRESS
If the protest committee decides to give redress by adjusting a boat's score for a race, it is advised to consider scoring her

(a) points equal to the average, to the nearest tenth of a point (0.05 to be rounded upward), of her points in all the races in the series except the race in question;

(b) points equal to the average, to the nearest tenth of a point (0.05 to be rounded upward), of her points in all the races before the race in question; or

(c) points based on the position of the boat in the race at the time of the incident that justified redress.

A11 SCORING ABBREVIATIONS
These abbreviations are recommended for recording the circumstances described:

DNC	Did not *start*; did not come to the starting area
DNS	Did not *start* (other than DNC and OCS)
OCS	Did not *start*; on the course side of the starting line and broke rule 29.1 or 30.1
ZFP	20% penalty under rule 30.2
BFD	Disqualification under rule 30.3
SCP	Took a scoring penalty under rule 44.3
DNF	Did not *finish*
RAF	Retired after *finishing*
DSQ	Disqualification
DNE	Disqualification not excludable under rule 88.3(b)
RDG	Redress given

APPENDIX B – SAILBOARD RACING RULES

Sailboard races shall be sailed under The Racing Rules of Sailing *as changed by this appendix.*

B1 DEFINITIONS
Add the following definitions:

Capsized A sailboard is *capsized* when her sail or the competitor's body is in the water.

Recovering A sailboard is *recovering* from the time her sail or, when water-starting, the competitor's body is out of the water until she has steerage way.

B2 PART 2 – WHEN BOATS MEET
B2.1 The last sentence of rule 20 is changed to: 'A sailboard moving astern shall *keep clear* of other sailboards and boats.'

B2.2 Add to Section D:

23 SAIL OUT OF THE WATER WHEN STARTING
When approaching the starting line to *start,* a sailboard shall have her sail out of the water and in a normal position, except when accidentally *capsized.*

24 RECOVERING
A sailboard *recovering* shall avoid a sailboard or boat under way.

B3 PART 3 – CONDUCT OF A RACE
Rule 31 is changed to: 'A competitor shall not hold on to a starting *mark.*'

B4 PART 4 – OTHER REQUIREMENTS WHEN RACING
B4.1 Rule 42 is changed to: 'A sailboard shall be propelled only by the action of the wind on the sail, by the action of the water on the hull

and by the unassisted actions of the competitor.'

B4.2 Rule 43.1(a) is modified to permit a competitor to wear a container for holding beverages. The container shall have a capacity of at least one litre and weigh no more than 1.5 kilograms when full.

B4.3 In rule 44.2, delete 'including two tack and two gybes'.

B5 PART 6 – ENTRY AND QUALIFICATION
Add to rule 78.1: 'When so prescribed by the national authority, a numbered and dated device on a sailboard and her daggerboard and sail shall serve as her measurement certificate.'

B6 PART 7 – RACE ORGANIZATION
In rule 88.2(c), the last sentence is changed to: 'Changes to the sailing instructions may be communicated orally, but only if the procedure is stated in the sailing instructions.'

B7 APPENDIX G – IDENTIFICATION ON SAILS
B7.1 Add to rule G1.1(a): 'The insignia shall not refer to anything other than the manufacturer or class and shall not consist of more than two letters and three numbers or an abstract design.'

B7.2 Rules G1.3(a), G1.3(c), G1.3(d) and G1.3(e) are changed to: 'The class insignia shall be displayed once on each side of the sail in the area above a line projected at right angles from a point on the luff of the sail one third of the distance from the head to the wishbone. The national letters and sail numbers shall be in the central third of the sail above the wishbone and clearly separated from any advertising and shall be placed at different heights on the two sides of the sail, those on the starboard side being uppermost.'

APPENDIX C – MATCH RACING RULES

Match races shall be sailed under The Racing Rules of Sailing *as changed by this appendix. Matches shall be umpired unless the notice of race and sailing instructions state otherwise.*

C1 TERMINOLOGY
'Competitor' means the skipper, team or boat as appropriate for the event. 'Flight' means two or more matches started in the same starting sequence.

C2 CHANGES TO THE DEFINITIONS AND THE RULES OF PART 2
C2.1 The definition *Finish* is changed to: 'A boat *finishes* when any part of her hull, crew or equipment in normal position, crosses the finishing line in the direction of the course from the last *mark* after completing any penalties. However, when penalties are cancelled under rule C7.2(d) after one or both boats have *finished* each shall be recorded as *finished* when she crossed the line.'

C2.2 Add to the definition *Proper Course*: 'A boat taking a penalty or manoeuvring to take a penalty is not sailing a *proper course.*'

C2.3 Change the last sentence of the definition *Clear Ahead* and *Clear Astern; Overlap* to: 'These terms do not apply to boats on opposite tacks unless either rule 18 applies or both boats are subject to rule 13.2.'

C2.4 Rule 13 becomes rule 13.1.

Add new rule 13.2: 'After the foot of the mainsail of a boat sailing down-wind crosses the centreline she shall *keep clear* until her mainsail has filled on the other *tack.*'

C2.5 Rules 16.2 and 17.2 are deleted.

C2.6 Rule 18.3 is changed to: 'If two boats were on opposite *tacks* and one of them completes a tack within the *two-length zone* to pass a *mark* or *obstruction,* and if thereafter the other boat cannot by luffing avoid becoming *overlapped* inside her, the boat that tacked shall *keep clear* and rules 15 and 18.2 do not apply. If the other boat can by luffing avoid becoming *overlapped* inside her then rule 18.2(c) shall apply as if the boats were *clear ahead* and *clear astern* at the *two-length zone.*'

C2.7 When rule 19.1 applies, the following arm signals by the helmsman are required in addition to the hails:

(a) for 'Room to tack', repeatedly and clearly pointing to windward; and

(b) for 'You tack', repeatedly and clearly pointing at the other boat and waving the arm to windward.

C2.8 In rule 20 the second sentence is changed to: 'A boat taking a penalty shall *keep clear* of one that is not.'

C2.9 Rule 22.1 is changed to: 'If reasonably possible, a boat not *racing* shall not interfere with a boat that is *racing* or an umpire boat.'

C2.10 Rule 22.2 is changed to: 'Except when sailing a *proper course*, a boat shall not interfere with a boat taking a penalty or sailing on another leg.'

C2.11 Add new rule 22.3: 'When boats in different matches meet, any change of course by either boat shall be consistent with complying with a *rule* or trying to win her own match.'

C3 RACE SIGNALS AND CHANGES TO RELATED RULES
C3.1 Starting Signals
The signals for starting a match shall be as follows. Times shall be taken from the visual signals; the failure of a sound signal shall be disregarded. If more than one match will be sailed, the starting signal for one match shall be the warning signal for the next match.

Time in minutes	Visual signal	Sound signal	Means
10	Flag F displayed	One	Attention
6	Flag F removed	None	
5	Numeral pennant displayed*	One	Warning signal
4	Flag P displayed	One	Preparatory signal
2	Blue or yellow flag or both displayed**	One**	End of pre-start entry time
0	Warning and preparatory signals removed	One	Starting signal

*Within a flight, numeral pennant 1 means Match 1, pennant 2 means Match 2, etc., unless the sailing instructions state otherwise.

**These signals shall be made only if one or both boats fail to comply with rule C4.2. The flag(s) shall be displayed until the umpires have signalled a penalty or for one minute, whichever is earlier.

C3.2 Changes to Related Rules
(a) Rule 29.1 is changed to: 'When at a boat's starting signal any part of her hull, crew or equipment is on the course side of the starting line or its extensions, she shall sail completely on the pre-start side of the line before *starting*.'

(b) Rule 29.2 is changed to: 'When at her starting signal a boat becomes subject to rule C3.2(a), the race committee shall promptly display a blue or yellow flag or both with one sound signal. Each flag shall be displayed until such boats are completely on the pre-start side of the starting line or its extensions or until two minutes after her starting signal, whichever is earlier.'

(c) When, after her starting signal, a boat sails on the course side of the starting line or its extensions, without having started correctly, the race committee shall promptly display a blue or yellow flag or both. Each flag shall be displayed until such boats are completely on the pre-start side of the starting line or its extensions or until two minutes after her starting signal, whichever is earlier.

(d) In Race Signal AP the last sentence is changed to: 'The attention signal will be made 1 minute after removal unless at that time the race is *postponed* again or *abandoned*.'

(e) In Race Signal N the last sentence is changed to: 'The attention signal will be made 1 minute after removal unless at that time the race is *abandoned* again or *postponed*.'

C3.3 Finishing Line Signals
The race signal 'Blue flag or shape' shall not be used.

C4 REQUIREMENTS BEFORE THE START
C4.1 At her preparatory signal, each boat shall be outside the line that is at 90° angle to the starting line through the starting *mark* at her assigned end. In the race schedule pairing list, the boat listed on the left-hand side is assigned the port end and shall display a blue flag at her stern while *racing*. The other boat is assigned the starboard end and shall display a yellow flag at her stern while *racing*.

C4.2 Within the two-minute period following her preparatory signal,

a boat shall cross and clear the starting line, the first time from the course side to the pre-start side.

C5 SIGNALS BY UMPIRES
(a) A green and white flag with one long sound signal means: 'No penalty.'

(b) A coloured flag identifying a boat with one long sound signal means: 'The identified boat shall take a penalty by complying with rule C7.'

(c) A red flag with or soon after a coloured flag with one long sound signal means: 'The identified boat shall take a penalty by complying with rule C7.3(d).'

(d) A black flag with a coloured flag and one long sound signal means: 'The identified boat is disqualified, and the match is terminated and awarded to the other boat.'

(e) One short sound signal means: 'A penalty is now completed.'

(f) Repetitive short sound signals mean: 'A boat is no longer taking a penalty and the penalty remains.'

(g) A coloured shape displayed from an umpire boat means: 'The identified boat has an outstanding penalty.'

C6 PROTESTS AND REQUESTS FOR REDRESS BY BOATS
C6.1 A boat may protest another boat

(a) under a rule of Part 2, except rule 14, by clearly displaying flag Y immediately after an incident in which she was involved.

(b) under any rule not listed in rule C6.1(a) or C6.2 by clearly displaying a red flag as soon as possible after the incident.

C6.2 A boat may not protest another boat under

(a) rule 14, unless damage results;

(b) a rule of Part 2, unless she was involved in the incident;

(c) rule 31 or 42; or

(d) rule C4 or C7.

C6.3 A boat intending to request redress because of circumstances that arise before she *finishes* or retires shall clearly display a red flag as soon as possible after she becomes aware of those circumstances, but not later than two minutes after *finishing* or retiring.

C6.4 (a) A boat protesting under rule C6.1(a) shall remove flag Y before or as soon as possible after the umpires' signal.

(b) A boat protesting under rule C6.1(b) or requesting redress under rule C6.3 shall, for her *protest* to be valid, keep her red flag displayed until she has so informed the umpires after *finishing* or retiring.

C 6.5 Umpire Decisions
After flag Y is displayed, the umpires shall decide whether to penalize any boat. They shall signal their decision in compliance with rule C5(a), (b) or (c).

C6.6 Protest Committee Decisions

(a) The protest committee may take evidence in any way it considers appropriate and may communicate its decision orally.

(b) If the protest committee decides that a breach of a *rule* has had no significant effect on the outcome of the match, it may

(1) impose a penalty of one point or part of one point,

(2) order a resail, or

(3) make another arrangement it decides is equitable, which may be to impose no penalty.

(c) The penalty for breaking rule 14 when damage results will be at the discretion of the protest committee, and may include exclusion from further races in the event.

C7 PENALTY SYSTEM
C7.1 Rule Changes
Rules 31.2 and 44 are deleted.

C7.2 All Penalties

(a) A penalized boat may delay taking a penalty within the limitations of rule C7.3 and shall take it as follows:

(1) When on a leg of the course to a windward *mark*, she shall gybe and, as soon as reasonably possible, luff to a close-hauled course.

(2) When on a leg of the course to a leeward *mark* or the finishing line, she shall *tack* and, as soon as reasonably possible, bear away to a down-wind course.

(b) Add to rule 2: 'When *racing*, a boat may wait for an umpire's decision before taking a penalty.'

(c) A boat completes a leg of the course when her bow crosses the extension of the line from the previous *mark* through the *mark* she is rounding, or on the last leg when she *finishes*.

(d) A penalized boat shall not be recorded as having *finished* until she takes her penalty and sails completely to the course side of the line and then *finishes*, unless the penalty is cancelled before or after she crosses the finishing line.

(e) If a boat has one or two outstanding penalties and the other boat in her match is penalized, one penalty for each boat shall be cancelled except that a 'red flag' penalty shall not cancel an outstanding penalty.

(f) If a boat has more than two outstanding penalties, the umpires shall signal her disqualification under rule C5(d).

C7.3 Penalty Limitations

(a) A boat taking a penalty that includes a tack shall have the spinnaker head below the main boom gooseneck from the time she passes head to wind until she is on a close-hauled course.

(b) No part of a penalty may be taken within two of a boat's hull lengths of a rounding *mark*.

(c) If a boat has one outstanding penalty, she may take the penalty any time after *starting* and before *finishing*. If a boat has two outstanding penalties, she shall take one of them as soon as reasonably possible, but not before *starting*.

(d) When the umpires display a red flag with or soon after a penalty flag, the penalized boat shall take a penalty as soon as reasonably possible, but not before *starting*. A 'red flag' penalty shall not cancel an outstanding penalty.

C7.4 Taking and Completing Penalties

(a) When a boat with an outstanding penalty is on a leg to a windward *mark* and gybes, or is on a leg to a leeward *mark* or the finishing line and passes head to wind, she is taking a penalty.

(b) When a boat taking a penalty either does not take the penalty correctly or does not complete the penalty as soon as reasonably possible, she is no longer taking a penalty. The umpires shall signal this as required by rule C5(f).

(c) The umpire boat for each match shall display coloured shapes, each shape indicating one outstanding penalty. When a boat has taken a penalty, or a penalty has been cancelled, one shape shall be removed. Failure of the umpires to display or remove shapes shall not change the number of penalties outstanding.

C8 PENALTIES INITIATED BY UMPIRES

C8.1 Rule Changes

(a) Rules 60.2(a) and 60.3(a) do not apply to rules for which penalties may be imposed by umpires.

(b) Rule 64.1(b) is changed so that the provision for exonerating a boat may be applied by the umpires without a hearing, and it takes precedence over any conflicting rule of this appendix.

C8.2 When the umpires decide that a boat has broken rule 31, 42, C4 or C7.3(c) she shall be penalized by signalling her under rule C5(b).

C8.3 When the umpires decide that a boat has

(a) gained an advantage by breaking a *rule* after allowing for a penalty,

(b) deliberately broken a *rule*, or

(c) committed a breach of sportsmanship,

she shall be penalized under rule C5(b) or C5(d).

C8.4 If the umpires or protest committee members decide that a boat may have broken a *rule* other than those listed in rule C6.1(a) or C6.2, they shall so inform the protest committee for its action under rule 60.3 and rule C6.6 when appropriate.

C8.5 When, after one boat has *started*, the umpires are satisfied that the other boat will not *start*, they may signal under rule C5(d) that the boat that did not *start* is disqualified and the match is terminated.

C9 REQUESTS FOR REDRESS OR REOPENINGS, APPEALS, OTHER PROCEEDINGS

C9.1 There shall be no request for redress or an appeal from a decision made under rule C5, C6, C7 or C8. In rule 66 the third sentence is changed to: 'A *party* to the hearing may not ask for a reopening.'

C9.2 A competitor may not base a request for redress on a claim that an action by an official boat was improper. The protest committee may decide to consider giving redress in such circumstances but only if it believes that an official boat, including an umpire boat, may have seriously interfered with a competing boat.

C9.3 No proceedings of any kind may be taken in relation to any action or non-action by the umpires, except as permitted in rule C9.2.

C10 SCORING

C10.1 The winning competitor of each match scores one point (half of one point each for a dead heat); the loser scores no points.

C10.2 When a competitor withdraws from part of an event the scores of all completed races shall stand.

C10.3 When a multiple round robin is terminated with an incomplete round robin, only one point shall be available for all the matches sailed between any two competitors, as follows:

Number of matches completed between any two competitors	Points for each win
1	One point
2	One-half point
3	One-third point

(etc.)

C10.4 In a round-robin series,

(a) competitors shall be placed in order of their total scores, highest score first;

(b) a competitor who has won a match but is disqualified for breaking a *rule* against a competitor in another match shall lose the point for that match (but the losing competitor shall not be awarded the point); and

(c) the overall position between competitors who have sailed in different groups shall be decided by the highest score.

C10.5 In a knockout series the sailing instructions shall prescribe the minimum number of points required to win a series between two competitors. When a knockout series is terminated it shall be decided in favour of the competitor with the higher score.

C11 TIES

C11.1 Round-Robin Series

A round-robin series means a grouping of competitors who all sail against each other one or more times. Each separate stage identified in the event format shall be a separate round-robin series irrespective of the number of times each competitor sails against each other competitor in that stage.

Ties between two or more competitors in a round-robin series shall be broken by the following methods, in order, until the tie is broken. When the tie is only partially broken, paragraphs (a) to (e) shall be reapplied to the remaining ties. The tie shall be decided in favour of the competitor(s) who

(a) placed in order, has the highest score in the matches between the tied competitors.

(b) when the tie is between two competitors in a multiple round robin, has won the last match between the two competitors.

(c) has the most points against the competitor placed highest in the round-robin series or, if necessary, second highest, and so on until the tie is broken.

When two separate ties have to be resolved but the resolution of each depends upon resolving the other, the following principles shall be used in the C11.1(c) procedure:

(1) the higher place tie shall be resolved before the lower place tie, and

(2) all the competitors in the lower place tie shall be treated as a single competitor for the purposes of rule C11.1(c).

(d) after applying rule C10.4(c), has the highest place in the different groups, irrespective of the number of competitors in each group.

(e) has the highest place in the most recent stage of the event (fleet race, round robin, etc.).

C11.2 Knockout Series
Ties (including 0–0) between two competitors in a knockout series shall be broken by the following methods, in order, until the tie is broken. The tie shall be decided in favour of the competitor who

(a) has the highest place in the most recent round-robin series, applying rule C11.1 if necessary.

(b) has won the most recent match in the event between the tied competitors.

C11.3 When rule C11.1 or C11.2 does not resolve the tie:

(a) If the tie needs to be resolved for a later stage of the event (or another event for which the event is a direct qualifier), the tie shall be broken by a sail-off when practicable. When the race committee decides a sail-off is not practicable the tie shall be broken by a draw.

(b) To decide the winner of an event, or the overall position between competitors eliminated in one round of a knockout series, a sail-off may be used (but not a draw).

(c) When a tie is not broken any monetary prizes or ranking points for tied places shall be added together and divided equally among the tied competitors.

Note: A Standard Notice of Race and Standard Sailing Instructions for match racing are available from the ISAF.

APPENDIX D – TEAM RACING RULES

Team races shall be sailed under The Racing Rules of Sailing *as changed by this appendix. If umpires or observers will be used the sailing instructions shall so state.*

D1 CHANGES TO THE RACING RULES
D1.1 The following rules are changed, added or deleted:

(a) Rule 17.2 is changed to: 'Except on a beat to windward, while a boat is less than two of her hull lengths from a *leeward* boat, she shall not sail below her *proper course* unless she gybes.'

(b) Rule 18.4 is deleted.

(c) Add to rule 22.2: 'Except when sailing a *proper course*, a boat shall not interfere with a boat on another leg or lap of the course. For the purpose of this rule, a boat that has *finished* is on a different leg from one that has not.'

(d) Add new rule 22.3: 'When boats in different races meet, any change of course by either boat shall be consistent with complying with a *rule* or trying to win her own race.'

(e) Add to rule 41: 'A boat that receives help from a team-mate does not break this rule.'

D1.2 The following additional rules apply:

(a) There shall be no penalty for breaking a rule of Part 2 when the incident is between boats in the same team and there is no contact.

(b) A boat damaged by a team-mate boat is not eligible for redress

based on that damage.

D2 INTENTION TO PROTEST; ACKNOWLEDGEMENT OF BREACHES OF RULES
D2.1 General
(a) A boat intending to protest shall hail the other boat immediately and promptly display a red flag.

(b) A boat that, while *racing*, may have broken a rule of Part 2, except rule 14 when the boat has caused damage, or rule D1 may take a penalty as provided by rules 44.1 and 44.2, except that only one turn is required. When an incident occurs at the finishing line or when an umpire's penalty is signalled at or beyond the finishing line, a boat shall not be recorded as having *finished* until she has completed her penalty and sailed completely to the course side of the line before *finishing*.

(c) When after displaying a red flag a boat is satisfied that the other boat has taken a penalty in compliance with rule D2.1(b) she shall remove her red flag.

(d) A boat that has displayed a red flag and then decides reasonably promptly that she, and not the other boat, was at fault shall immediately remove her flag, take a penalty in compliance with rule D2.1(b), and hail the other boat accordingly.

(e) The sailing instructions may state that rule D2.2(g) applies to all *protests*.

D2.2 Umpired Races
Races to be umpired shall be identified either in the sailing instructions or by the display of flag U no later than the warning signal.

(a) When a boat protests under a rule of Part 2, except rule 14, or under rule D1, 31.1, 42 or 44, she is not entitled to a hearing. Instead, when the protested boat fails either to acknowledge breaking a *rule* or to take a penalty in compliance with rule D2.1(b) the protesting boat may display a yellow flag and request a decision by hailing 'Umpire'.

(b) An umpire shall signal a decision as follows:

(1) A green flag or a green and white flag means 'No penalty imposed; incident closed'.

(2) A red flag means 'One or more boats are penalized.' The umpire shall hail or signal to identify each boat to be penalized.

The protesting boat shall then remove her flag.

(c) A boat penalized by an umpire's decision shall make two 360° turns (720°) in compliance with rule 44.2.

(d) When a boat commits a breach of sportsmanship or fails to take a penalty when required by an umpire, or when a boat or her team gains an advantage despite taking a penalty, an umpire may impose one or more 360° turn penalties by displaying a red flag and hailing her accordingly, or report the incident as provided in rule D2.2(e).

(e) When an incident involves reckless sailing, rule 14 when damage may have been caused, rule 28.1 or failure to comply with an umpire's decision, the umpire may report the incident to a protest committee which may further penalize the boat concerned. The umpire shall signal this intention by displaying a black flag and hailing appropriately.

(f) Rules 60.2 and 60.3 do not apply. The protest committee may call a hearing only on receipt of a report from an umpire as provided in rule D2.2(e) or under rule 69.

(g) *Protests* need not be in writing, and the protest committee may take evidence in any way it considers appropriate and may communicate its decision orally.

(h) There shall be no requests for redress or to reopen a hearing or appeals by a boat arising from decisions or actions or non-actions by the umpires. The protest committee may decide to consider giving redress when it believes that an official boat, including an umpire boat, may have seriously interfered with a competing boat.

D2.3 Races with Observers
Observers may be appointed by the race committee to observe the racing and give opinions on incidents when requested. If so, rule D2.2 applies except that

(a) a boat need not request an opinion or accept one, in which case any *protest* shall comply with and be decided under the rules of Part 5 as changed by this appendix;

(b) an observer may display a yellow flag to signal that he has no opinion. If a boat then intends to protest she may do so by complying with the rules of Part 5 as changed by this appendix.

D3 SCORING A RACE

D3.1 (a) Each boat *finishing* a race, whether or not rules 28.1 and 29.1 have been complied with, shall be scored points equal to her finishing place. All other boats shall be scored points equal to the number of boats entitled to *race*.

(b) In addition, a boat's score shall be increased as follows:

Rule broken	Penalty points
(1)rule 14 when the boat has caused damage, or rule 29.1	10
(2)any other rule for which a penalty has not been taken	6

However, a boat that breaks rule 28.1 and does not *finish* shall not have the penalty points in (2) above added to her score for this breach when it gained neither her nor her team any advantage. The protest committee may further increase a boat's score when she has broken a *rule* and as a result her team has gained an advantage.

(c) The team with the lowest total points wins. If there is a tie on points, the team having the combination of race scores that does not include a first place wins.

D3.2 When all boats of one team have *finished* or retired, the race committee may stop the race. The other team's boats shall be scored the points they would have received had they *finished*.

D3.3 When all the boats of a team fail to *start* in a race, each shall be scored points equal to the number of boats entitled to *race*, and the boats of the other team shall be scored as if they had *finished* in the best positions.

D4 SCORING A SERIES

D4.1 A team racing series shall consist of races or matches. A match shall consist of two races between the same two teams. The team with the lower total points for the race or the match wins.

D4.2 When two or more teams are competing in a series consisting of races or matches, the series winner shall be the team winning the greatest number of races or matches. The other teams shall be ranked in order of number of wins. Tied matches shall count as half a win to each team.

D4.3 When necessary, ties in a completed series shall be broken using, in order of precedence,

(a) the number of races or matches won when the tied teams met;

(b) the points scored when the tied teams met;

(c) if two teams remain tied, the last race between them;

(d) total points scored in all races against common opponents;

(e) a game of chance.

If a multiple tie is only partially resolved by one of these, then the remaining tie shall be broken by starting again at rule D4.3(a).

D4.4 If a series is not completed, teams shall be ranked according to the results from completed rounds, and ties shall be broken initially using the results from races or matches between the tied teams in the incomplete round. If no round has been completed, teams shall be ranked in order of their race (or match) win-loss ratios. Thereafter, rule D4.3(a) to D4.3(e) shall be used to break ties.

D5 BREAKDOWNS WHEN BOATS ARE SUPPLIED BY THE ORGANIZING AUTHORITY

D5.1 A supplied boat suffering a breakdown shall display a red flag as soon as practicable and, if possible, continue *racing*.

D5.2 When the race committee decides that the boat's finishing position was made significantly worse, that the breakdown was not the fault of the crew, and that in the same circumstances a reasonably competent crew would not have been able to avoid the breakdown, it shall make as

equitable a decision as possible, which may be to order the race to be resailed or, when the boat's *finishing* position was predictable, award her points for that position. In case of doubt about her position when she broke down, the doubt shall be resolved against her.

D5.3 A breakdown caused by defective supplied equipment or a breach of a *rule* by an opponent shall not normally be determined to be the fault of the crew, but one caused by careless handling, capsizing or a breach by a boat of the same team shall be. Any doubt about the fault of the crew shall be resolved in the boat's favour.

APPENDIX E – RADIO-CONTROLLED BOAT RACING RULES

Races for radio-controlled boats shall be sailed under The Racing Rules of Sailing *as changed by this appendix.*

E1 TERMINOLOGY, RACE SIGNALS, DEFINITIONS AND FUNDAMENTAL RULES

E1.1 Terminology
'Boat' means a boat that is radio-controlled by a competitor who is not on board. For 'race' used as a noun outside this appendix and Appendix A read 'heat'. Within this appendix, a race consists of one or more heats, and is completed when the last heat in the race is finished. An 'event' consists of one or more races. A 'series' consists of a specified number of races or events.

E1.2 Race Signals
Race Signals do not apply. All signals shall be given orally or by other sounds described in this appendix.

E1.3 Definitions
(a) Add to the definition *Interested Party* 'but not a competitor when acting as an observer'.

(b) In the definition *Two-Length Zone* change '*Two*' to '*Four*'.

E1.4 Personal Buoyancy
Rule 1.2 is replaced with 'When on board a rescue vessel, each competitor shall be responsible for wearing personal buoyancy adequate for the conditions.'

E1.5 Aerials
Transmitter aerial extremities shall be adequately protected. When a protest committee finds that a competitor has broken this rule it shall either warn him and give him time to comply or penalize him.

E2 PART 2 – WHEN BOATS MEET
Rule 21 is replaced with:

Capsized or Entangled

If possible, a boat shall avoid a boat that is capsized or entangled, or has not regained control after capsizing or entanglement. A boat is capsized when her masthead is in the water. Two or more boats are entangled when lying together for a period of time so that no boat is capable of manoeuvring to break free of the other(s).

E3 PART 3 – CONDUCT OF A RACE
E3.1 Races with Observers
The race committee may appoint race observers, who may be competitors. They shall remain in the control area, while boats are *racing* and they shall hail and repeat the identity of boats that contact a *mark* or another boat. Such hails shall be made from the control area. Observers shall report all unresolved incidents to the race committee at the end of the heat.

E3.2 Course Board
Rule J2.1(3) does not apply. A course board showing the course and the limits of the control area and launching area(s) shall be located next to or within the control area with information clearly visible to competitors while *racing*.

E3.3 Control and Launching Areas
The control and launching area(s) shall be defined by the sailing instructions. Competitors *racing* shall remain in the control area while a heat is in progress, except that competitors may briefly go to and return from the launching area to perform functions permitted in rule E4.5. Competitors not *racing* shall remain outside the control and launching areas except when offering assistance under rule E4.2 or when acting as race observers.

E3.4 Non-applicable Rules
The second sentence of rule 25 and all of rule 33 do not apply.

E3.5 Starting Races
Rule 26 is replaced with:

'Audible signals for starting a heat shall be at one-minute intervals and shall be a warning signal, a preparatory signal and a starting signal. During the minute before the starting signal, verbal signals shall be made at ten-second intervals, and during the final ten seconds at one-second intervals. The start shall be at the beginning of the starting signal.'

E3.6 Starting Penalties
In rules 29.1 and 30 delete the word 'crew'. Throughout rule 30 oral announcements shall replace the display of flag signals.

E3.7 Starting and Finishing Lines
The starting and finishing lines shall be tangential to, and on the course side of, the starting and finishing *marks*.

E3.8 Individual Recall
Rule 29.2 is changed. Delete all after 'the race committee shall promptly' and replace with 'twice hail "Recall (sail numbers)"'.

E3.9 General Recall
Rule 29.3 is changed. Delete all after 'the race committee may' and replace with 'twice hail "General recall" with two sound signals'. After the recalled start, the warning signal for a new start shall be made.

E3.10 Shortening or Abandoning after the Start
In rule 32.1(b) delete 'foul weather' and replace with 'thunderstorms'. Rules 32.1(c) and 32.2 do not apply.

E4 PART 4 – OTHER REQUIREMENTS WHEN RACING

E4.1 Non-applicable rules
Rules 42.2(b), 42.2(c), 42.3(a), 42.3(c), 43, 47, 48, 49, 50, 52 and 54 do not apply.

E4.2 Outside Help
Rule 41 is replaced with:

(a) A competitor shall not give tactical or strategic advice to a competitor who is *racing*.

(b) A competitor who is *racing* shall not receive outside help except:
    (1) A boat that has gone ashore or aground outside the launching area, or become entangled with another boat or *mark*, may be freed and relaunched only with outside help from a rescue vessel crew.

    (2) Competitors who are not *racing* and others may give outside help in the launching area as permitted by rule E4.5.

E4.3 Propulsion and Prohibited Actions
(a) In rule 42.1 delete all after 'sails and hull'.

(b) In rule 42.2(a) delete all after 'releasing the sail'.

E4.4 Penalties for Breaking a Rule of Part 2
Throughout rule 44 the penalty shall be one 360° turn, including one *tack* and one gybe.

E4.5 Launching and Relaunching
Rule 45 is replaced with:

(a) Except between the preparatory and starting signals, boats scheduled to race in a heat may be launched, taken ashore or relaunched at any time during the heat.

(b) Boats shall be launched or recovered only from within a launching area, except as provided by rule E4.2(b)(1).

(c) While ashore or within a launching area, boats may be adjusted, drained of water, or repaired; have their sails changed or reefed; have entangled objects removed; or have radio equipment repaired or changed.

E4.6 Person in Charge
Rule 46 is changed. Delete 'have on board' and replace with 'be radio- controlled by'.

E4.7 Moving Ballast
Rule 51 is replaced with:

During an event and unless class rules specify otherwise,

(a) ballast shall not be shifted, shipped or unshipped;

(b) except for replacements of similar weight and position, no control equipment shall be shifted, shipped or unshipped;

(c) the position of rig counterbalance weights may be adjusted; and

(d) bilge water shall not be used to trim the boat, but may be removed at any time.

E4.8 Radio
(a) A competitor shall not transmit radio signals that cause interference with the radio reception of other boats.

(b) A competitor found to have broken rule E4.8(a) shall not race until he has proven compliance with rule E4.8(a).

E4.9 Boat Out of Radio Control
A competitor who loses radio control of his boat shall promptly hail and repeat 'Out of control (the boat's sail number)'. Such a boat shall be deemed to have retired and shall be considered an *obstruction*.

E5 PART 5 – PROTESTS, REDRESS, HEARINGS, MISCONDUCT AND APPEALS
E5.1 Right to Protest and Request Redress
Add to rule 60.1(a): 'A *protest* alleging a breach of a rule of Part 2, 3 or 4 shall be made only by a competitor within the control or launching area and by a boat scheduled to *race* in the heat in which the incident occurred.' After the words 'report by a competitor from another boat' in rules 60.2(a) and 60.3(a) add 'except when acting as an observer'.

E5.2 Informing the Protestee
In rule 61.1(a) delete all after the first sentence and replace with 'When her *protest* concerns an incident in the racing area that she is involved in or sees, she shall twice hail '(Her own sail number) "protest" (the sail number of the other boat).'

E5.3 Protest Time Limit
In rule 61.3 delete 'two hours' and replace with '15 minutes'. Add 'A protestor intending to submit a *protest* shall inform the race committee within five minutes of the end of the relevant heat.'

E5.4 Accepting Responsibility
A boat that acknowledges breaking a rule of Part 2, 3 or 4 before the *protest* is found to be valid may retire from the relevant heat without further penalty.

E5.5 Redress
(a) Add to rule 62.1:

(e) radio interference, or

(f) an entanglement or grounding because of the action of a boat that was breaking a rule of Part 2 or of a vessel not *racing* that was required to *keep clear*.
(b) The first sentence of rule 62.2 is changed to 'The request shall be made in writing within the time limit of rule E5.3.'

E5.6 Right to Be Present
In rule 63.3(a) delete 'shall have been on board' and replace with 'shall have been radio-controlling them'.

E5.7 Taking Evidence and Finding Facts
Add to rule 63.6: 'Evidence about an alleged breach of a rule of Part 2, 3 or 4 given by competitors shall be accepted only from a competitor who was within the control or launching area and whose boat was scheduled to *race* in the heat in which the incident occurred.'

E5.8 Penalties and Exoneration
Instead of disqualification as provided by rule 64.1(a), the penalty for breaking rule E3.3, E4.2(a) or E4.5 may be determined by the protest committee to be

(a) exclusion from the next race,

(b) disqualification from the next race, or

(c) one or more penalty turns that must be taken immediately after the boat has started her next race.

In these cases rule 64.1(c) does not apply.

E5.9 Decision on Redress
Add to rule 64.2: 'If a boat given redress was damaged, she shall be given reasonable time, but not more than 30 minutes, to effect repairs before her next heat.'

E5.10 Reopening a Hearing
In rule 66 '24 hours' is changed to 'ten minutes'.

E6 APPENDIX G – IDENTIFICATION ON SAILS

Appendix G is changed as follows:

(a) In rule G1 add 'RSD' after 'ISAF'.

(b) Rule G1.1(c) is replaced by: 'a sail number, which shall be the last two digits of the boat registration number, allotted by the relevant issuing authority.' Where this is a single-digit number, a '0' shall be placed in front. Alternatively an owner may be allotted a personal sail number by the relevant issuing authority, the last two digits of which may be used on all his boats. Where this is a single-digit number, a '0' shall be placed in front.

(c) In rule G1.2(b) delete 'and opposite' and add to the table:

	Minimum height	Minimum space between letters and numerals or edge of sail
numbers on RC boats	100 mm	13 mm
letters on RC boats	60 mm	13 mm

Maximum dimensions shall be the minimum plus 10 mm. The space between marks on opposite sides of the sail shall be 60–100 mm. If a sail is too small to use the specified dimensions, smaller letters and numbers may be used, with 13 mm as the absolute minimum spacing.

(d) Rule G1.3(c) is replaced by: 'Sail numbers shall be placed above the national letters. There shall be space in front of the sail number for the prefix '1', which may be prescribed by the race committee in the event of a conflict between numbers.'

(e) Rule G1.3(e) is replaced by: 'The sail number shall be displayed on both sides of the headsail.

APPENDIX F – APPEALS PROCEDURES

See rule 70. A national authority may change this appendix by prescription but it shall not be changed by sailing instructions.

F1 NATIONAL AUTHORITY
Appeals, requests by protest committees for confirmation or correction of decisions, and requests for the interpretation of *rules* shall be made to the national authority.

F2 APPELLANT'S RESPONSIBILITIES
F2.1 Within 15 days of receiving the protest committee's written decision or its decision not to reopen a hearing, the appellant shall send a dated appeal to the national authority with a copy of the protest committee's decision. The appeal shall state why the appellant believes the protest committee's interpretation of a *rule* or its procedures were incorrect.

F2.2 The appellant shall also send, with the appeal or as soon as possible thereafter, any of the following documents that are available to her:

(a) the written *protest(s)* or request(s) for redress;

(b) a diagram, prepared or endorsed by the protest committee, showing the positions and tracks of all boats involved, the course to the next *mark* and the required side, the force and direction of the wind, and, if relevant, the depth of water and direction and speed of any current;

(c) the notice of race, the sailing instructions, any other conditions governing the event, and any changes to them;

(d) any additional relevant documents; and

(e) the names and addresses of all *parties* to the hearing and the protest committee chairman.

F2.3 A request from a protest committee for confirmation or correction

of its decision shall include the decision and all relevant documents. A request for a *rule* interpretation shall include assumed facts.

F3 NOTIFICATION AND RESPONSE OF THE PROTEST COMMITTEE
Upon receipt of an appeal, the national authority shall send a copy of the appeal to the protest committee, asking the protest committee for the documents listed in rule F2.2 not supplied by the appellant, and the protest committee shall send the documents to the national authority.

F4 NATIONAL AUTHORITY'S RESPONSIBILITIES
The national authority shall send copies of the appeal and the protest committee's decision to the other *parties* to the hearing. It shall send to the appellant copies of documents not sent by the appellant. It shall send to any *party* to the hearing upon request any of the documents listed in rule F2.2.

F5 ADDITIONAL INFORMATION
The national authority shall accept the protest committee's finding of facts except when it decides they are inadequate, in which case it may require the protest committee to provide additional facts or other information, or to reopen the hearing and report any new finding of facts.

F6 COMMENTS
Parties to the hearing and the protest committee may send comments on the appeal to the national authority, provided they do so within 15 days of receiving the appeal. The national authority shall send such comments to all *parties* to the hearing and to the protest committee.

F7 WITHDRAWING AN APPEAL
An appellant may withdraw an appeal before it is decided by accepting the protest committee's decision.

APPENDIX G
– IDENTIFICATION ON SAILS

See rule 77.

G1 ISAF INTERNATIONAL CLASS BOATS
G1.1 Identification
Every boat of an ISAF International Class or Recognized Class shall carry on her mainsail and, as provided in rules G1.3(d) and G1.3(e) for letters and numbers only, on her spinnaker and headsail

(a) the insignia denoting her class;

(b) at all international events, except when the boats are provided to all competitors, national letters denoting her national authority from the table below. For the purposes of this rule, international events are ISAF events, world and continental championships, and events described as international events in their notices of race and sailing instructions; and

(c) a sail number of no more than four digits allotted by her national authority or, when so required by the class rules, by the international class association. The four-digit limitation does not apply to classes whose ISAF membership or recognition took effect before 1 April 1997. Alternatively, if permitted in the class rules, an owner may be allotted a personal sail number by the relevant issuing authority, which may be used on all his boats in that class.

Sails measured before 31 March 1999 shall comply with rule G1.1 or with the rules applicable at the time of measurement.

Letters	National authority	Letters	National authority
ALG	Algeria	ASA	American Samoa
AND	Andorra	ANG	Angola
ANT	Antigua	ARG	Argentina
ARM	Armenia	AUS	Australia
AUT	Austria	BAH	Bahamas
BRN	Bahrain	BAR	Barbados
BLR	Belarus	BEL	Belgium
BER	Bermuda	BRA	Brazil
IVB	British Virgin Islands	BRU	Brunei Darussalam
BUL	Bulgaria	CAN	Canada
CHI	Chile	CHN	China
TPE	Chinese Taipei	COL	Columbia
COK	Cook Islands	CRO	Croatia
CUB	Cuba	CYP	Cyprus
CZE	Czech Republic	DEN	Denmark
DOM	Dominican Republic	ECU	Ecuador
EGY	Egypt	ESA	El Salvador

EST	Estonia	FIJ	Fiji
FIN	Finland	FRA	France
GAB	Gabon	GEO	Georgia
GER	Germany	CAY	Grand Cayman
GBR	Great Britain	GRE	Greece
GRN	Grenada	GUM	Guam
GUA	Guatemala	HKG	Hong Kong
HUN	Hungary	ISL	Iceland
IND	India	INA	Indonesia
IRL	Ireland	ISR	Israel
ITA	Italy	JAM	Jamaica
JPN	Japan	KAZ	Kazakhstan
KEN	Kenya	KOR	Korea
KUW	Kuwait	KGZ	Kyrghyzstan
LAT	Latvia	LIB	Lebanon
LBA	Libya	LIE	Liechtenstein
LTU	Lithuania	LUX	Luxembourg
MAS	Malaysia	MLT	Malta
MRI	Mauritius	MEX	Mexico
FSM	Micronesia	MDA	Moldova
MON	Monaco	MAR	Morocco
MYA	Myanmar	NAM	Namibia
NED	The Netherlands	AHO	Netherlands Antilles
NZL	New Zealand	NGR	Nigeria
NOR	Norway	PAK	Pakistan
PNG	Papua New Guinea	PAR	Paraguay
PER	Peru	PHI	Philippines
POL	Poland	POR	Portugal
PUR	Puerto Rico	QAT	Qatar
ROM	Romania	RUS	Russia
SMR	San Marino	SEY	Seychelles
SIN	Singapore	SVK	Slovak Republic
SLO	Slovenia	RSA	South Africa
ESP	Spain	SRI	Sri Lanka
LCA	St. Lucia	SUD	Sudan
SWE	Sweden	SUI	Switzerland
TAH	Tahiti	THA	Thailand
TRI	Trinidad & Tobago	TUN	Tunisia
TUR	Turkey	UKR	Ukraine
UAE	United Arab Emirates	USA	United States of America
URU	Uruguay	ISV	US Virgin Islands
UZB	Uzbekistan	VEN	Venezuela
YUG	Yugoslavia	ZIM	Zimbabwe

G1.2 Specifications

(a) National letters and sail numbers shall be in capital letters and Arabic numerals, clearly legible and of the same colour. Commercially available typefaces giving the same or better legibility than Helvetica are acceptable.

(b) The sizes of characters and minimum space between adjoining characters on the same and opposite sides of the sail shall be related to the boat's overall length as follows:

Overall length	Minimum height	Minimum space between letters and numerals or edge of sail
under 3.5 m	230 mm	45 mm
3.5 m – 8.5 m	300 mm	60 mm
8.5 m – 11 m	375 mm	75 mm
over 11 m	450 mm	90 mm

G1.3 Positioning

Class insignia, national letters and sail numbers shall be positioned as follows:

(a) Except as provided in (d) and (e) below, class insignia, national letters and sail numbers shall when possible be wholly above an arc whose centre is the head point and whose radius is 60% of the leech length. They shall be placed at different heights on the two sides of the sail, those on the starboard side being uppermost.

(b) The class insignia shall be placed above the national letters. If the class insignia is of such a design that two of them coincide when placed back to back on both sides of the sail, they may be so placed.

(c) National letters shall be placed above the sail number.

(d) The national letters and sail number shall be displayed on the front side of a spinnaker but may be placed on both sides. They shall be

displayed wholly below an arc whose centre is the head point and whose radius is 40% of the foot median and, when possible, wholly above an arc whose radius is 60% of the foot median.

(e) The national letters and sail number shall be displayed on both sides of a headsail whose clew can extend behind the mast 30% or more of the mainsail foot length. They shall be displayed wholly below an arc whose centre is the head point and whose radius is half the luff length and, if possible, wholly above an arc whose radius is 75% of the luff length.

G2 OTHER BOATS

Other boats shall comply with the rules of their national authority or class association in regard to the allotment, carrying and size of insignia, letters and numbers. Such rules shall, when practicable, conform to the above requirements.

G3 CHARTERED OR LOANED BOATS

When so stated in the notice of race or sailing instructions, a boat chartered or loaned for an event may carry national letters or a sail number in contravention of her class rules.

G4 WARNINGS AND PENALTIES

When a protest committee finds that a boat has broken a rule of this appendix it shall either warn her and give her time to comply or penalize her.

G5 CHANGES BY CLASS RULES

ISAF classes may change the rules of this appendix provided the changes have first been approved by the ISAF.

APPENDIX H – WEIGHING CLOTHING AND EQUIPMENT

See Rule 43. This appendix shall not be changed by sailing instructions or prescriptions of national authorities.

H1 Items of clothing and equipment to be weighed shall be arranged on a rack. After being saturated in water the items shall be allowed to drain freely for one minute before being weighed. The rack must allow the items to hang as they would hang from clothes hangers, so as to allow the water to drain freely. Pockets that have drain-holes that cannot be closed shall be empty, but pockets or items that can hold water shall be full.

H2 When the weight recorded exceeds the amount permitted, the competitor may rearrange the items on the rack and the measurer shall again soak and weigh them. This procedure may be repeated a second time if the weight still exceeds the amount permitted.

H3 A competitor wearing a dry-suit may choose an alternative means of weighing the items.

(a) The dry-suit and items of clothing and equipment that are worn outside the dry-suit shall be weighed as described above.

(b) Clothing worn underneath the dry-suit shall be weighed as worn while *racing*, without draining.

(c) The two weights shall be added together.

APPENDIX J – NOTICE OF RACE AND SAILING INSTRUCTIONS

See rules 87.2 and 88.2(a). The term 'race' includes a regatta or other series of races.

J1 NOTICE OF RACE CONTENTS
J1.1 The notice of race shall include the following information:

(1) the title, place and dates of the race and name of the organizing authority;

(2) that the race will be governed by the *rules* as defined in *The Racing Rules of Sailing*;

(3) a list of any other documents that will govern the event (for example, the *Equipment Rules of Sailing*, to the extent that they apply);

(4) the classes to race, conditions of entry and any restrictions on entries;

(5) the times of registration and warning signals for the practice race or first race, and succeeding races if known.

J1.2 The notice of race shall include any of the following that would help competitors decide whether to attend the event or that conveys other information they will need before the sailing instructions become available:

(1) that advertising will be restricted to Category A (see Appendix 1) and other information related to Appendix 1;

(2) that the ISAF Competitor Classification System (or some other competitor classification system) will apply;

(3) the procedure for advance registration or entry, including fees and any closing dates;

(4) an entry form, to be signed by the boat's owner or owner's representative, containing words such as 'I agree to be bound by *The Racing Rules of Sailing* and by all other *rules* that govern this event';

(5) measurement procedures or requirements for measurement or rating certificates;

(6) the time and place at which the sailing instructions will be available;

(7) any changes to the racing rules (see rule 86);

(8) any changes to class rules, referring specifically to each rule and stating the change;

(9) the courses to be sailed;

(10) the penalty for breaking a rule of Part 2, other than the 720° Turns Penalty;

(11) denial of the right of appeal, subject to rule 70.4;

(12) the scoring system, including the number of races scheduled and the minimum number that must be completed to constitute a series;

(13) prizes.

J2 SAILING INSTRUCTION CONTENTS
J2.1 The sailing instructions shall include the following information:

(1) that the race will be governed by the rules as defined in *The Racing Rules of Sailing*;

(2) a list of any other documents that will govern the event (for example, the *Equipment Rules of Sailing*, to the extent that they apply);

(3) the schedule of races, the classes to race and times of warning signals for each class;

(4) the course(s) to be sailed, or a list of *marks* from which the course will be selected and, if relevant, how courses will be signalled;

(5) descriptions of *marks*, including starting and finishing *marks*, stating the order and side on which each is to be left and identifying all rounding *marks* (see rule 28.1);

(6) descriptions of the starting and finishing lines, class flags and any special signals to be used;

(7) the time limit, if any, for *finishing*;

(8) the scoring system, included by reference to Appendix A, to class rules or other rules governing the event, or stated in full. State the number of races scheduled and the minimum number that must be completed to constitute a series.

J2.2 The sailing instructions shall include those of the following that will apply:

(1) that advertising will be restricted to Category A (see Appendix 1) and other information related to Appendix 1;

(2) that the ISAF Competitor Classification System (or some other competitor classification system) will apply;

(3) replacement of the relevant rules of Part 2 with the *International Regulations for Preventing Collisions at Sea* or other government right-of-way rules, the time(s) or place(s) they will apply, and any night signals to be used by the race committee;

(4) changes to the *racing* rules permitted by rule 86, referring specifically to each rule and stating the change;

(5) that the prescriptions of the national authority will not apply;

(6) if the prescriptions of the national authority will apply at an international event, a copy in English of the prescriptions;

(7) changes to class rules, referring specifically to each rule and stating the change;

(8) restrictions controlling changes to boats when supplied by the organizing authority;

(9) the registration procedure;

(10) measurement or inspection procedure;

(11) location(s) of official notice board(s);

(12) procedure for changing the sailing instructions;

(13) safety requirements, such as requirements and signals for personal buoyancy, check-in at starting area, and check-out and check-in ashore;

(14) declaration requirements;

(15) signals to be made ashore and location of signal station(s);

(16) the racing area (a chart is recommended);

(17) approximate course length and approximate length of windward legs;

(18) the time limit, if any, for boats other than the first boat to *finish*;

(19) time allowances;

(20) the location of the starting area and any applicable restrictions;

(21) any special procedures or signals for individual or general recalls;

(22) boats identifying *mark* locations;

(23) procedure for changes of course after the start and any special signals;

(24) any special procedure for shortening the course or for *finishing* a shortened course;

(25) restrictions on use of support boats, plastic pools, radios, etc.; on hauling out; and on outside assistance provided to a boat that is not *racing*;

(26) the penalty for breaking a rule of Part 2, other than the 720° Turns Penalty;

(27) penalization without a hearing under rule 67 for breaking rule 42;

(28) whether Appendix N will apply;

(29) *protest* procedure and times and place of hearings;

(30) if rule M1.4(b) will apply, the time limit for requesting a hearing under that rule;

(31) denial of the right of appeal, subject to rule 70.4;

(32) the national authority's approval of the appointment of an international jury under rule 89(c);

(33) substitution of competitors;

(34) the minimum number of boats appearing in the starting area required for a race to be started;

(35) when and where races *postponed* or *abandoned* for the day will be resailed;

(36) tides and currents;

(37) prizes;

(38) other commitments of the race committee and obligations of boats.

APPENDIX K – SAILING INSTRUCTIONS GUIDE - not shown

APPENDIX L – RECOMMENDATIONS FOR PROTEST COMMITTEES - not shown

APPENDIX M – INTERNATIONAL JURIES - not shown

APPENDIX N – IMMEDIATE PENALTIES FOR BREAKING RULE 42

This appendix applies only if the sailing instructions so state.

N1 PROTESTS
A member of the protest committee or its designated observer who sees a boat breaking rule 42 may protest her by, as soon as reasonably possible, making a sound signal, pointing a yellow flag at her and hailing her sail number, even if she is no longer *racing*. A boat so protested is not subject to another *protest* under rule 42 for the same incident.

N2 PENALTIES
N2.1 First Protest
When a boat is first *protest*ed under rule N1 she may acknowledge her breach by taking a 720° Turns Penalty under rule 44.2. If she fails to do so she shall be disqualified without a hearing.

N2.2 Second Protest
When a boat is protested a second time during the series she may acknowledge her breach by immediately retiring from the race. If she fails to do so she shall be disqualified without a hearing and her score shall not be excluded.

N2.3 Third Protest
When a boat is protested a third time during the series she may acknowledge her breach by immediately retiring from the race and from all other races in the series. If she fails to do so she shall be disqualified without a hearing from all races in the series, with no score excluded, and the protest committee shall consider calling a hearing under rule 69.1(a).

N3 POSTPONEMENT, GENERAL RECALL OR ABANDONMENT
If a boat has been protested under rule N1 and the race committee signals a *postponement,* general recall or a*bandonment,* the penalty from her first or second *protest* is cancelled, but the *protest* is counted to determine the number of times she has been protested during the series.

APPENDICES, SECTION II

The appendices of this Section, which are both ISAF regulations and racing rules, may be amended or changed at any meeting of the ISAF Council. Any amendment or change will be posted on the ISAF website (www.sailing.org) as soon as practicable and may be obtained directly from the ISAF.

APPENDIX 1 – ISAF ADVERTISING CODE

REGULATION 20
See rule 79. This appendix shall not be changed by sailing instructions or prescriptions of national authorities. When governmental requirements conflict with parts of it, those requirements apply to the extent that they are more restrictive.

20. ADVERTISING CODE

20.1 *Definition of Advertising*
For the purposes of this code, advertising is the name, logo, slogan, description, depiction, a variation or distortion thereof, or any other form of communication that promotes an organization, person, product, service, brand or idea so as to call attention to it or to persuade persons or organizations to buy, approve or otherwise support it.

20.2. *General*

20.2.1 Advertising shall not be displayed on a boat, except as required or permitted by the ISAF Advertising Code.

20.2.2 Advertisements and anything advertised shall meet generally accepted moral and ethical standards.

20.2.3 Advertisements on sails shall be clearly separated from national

letters and sail numbers.

20.3. *Advertising*

20.3.1 The following types of advertising are permitted or required as stated and apply at all times:

(a) Boats and Sailboards

The class insignia shall be displayed on her sails as required by RRS Appendix G.

(b) (i) Boats

One sailmaker's mark, which may include the name or mark of the sailcloth manufacturer and the pattern or model of the sail, may be displayed on both sides of any sail and shall fit within a 150mm x 150mm square. On sails, other than spinnakers, no part of such mark shall be placed farther from the tack point than the greater of 300mm or 15% of the length of the foot.

(ii) Sailboards

One sailmaker's mark, which may include the name or mark of the sailcloth manufacturer and the pattern or model of the sail, may be displayed on both sides of the sail and shall fit within a 150mm x 150mm square. No part of such mark shall be placed farther from the tack point than 20% of the length of the foot of the sail, including the mast sleeve. The mark may also be displayed on the lower half of the part of the sail above the wishbone (boom) but no part of it shall be farther than 500mm from the clew point.

(c) (i) Boats

One builder's mark, which may include the name or mark of the designer, may be placed on the hull, and one maker's mark may be displayed on each side on spars and on each side of other equipment. Such marks shall fit within a 150mm x 150mm square.

(ii) Sailboards

Any number of manufacturers' names or logos may be placed on the board (hull) and in two places on the upper third of the part of the sail above the wishbone (boom). One maker's mark may be displayed each side on spars, and on each side of any other equipment.

(d) (i) Boats

The forward part of the hull on each side of all participating boats in an event shall only display advertising chosen and required to be displayed by that event organizer as follows:

- for boats under 6.5 metres, 25% of the *hull length*, and
- for boats over 6.5 metres, 20% of the *hull length*

excluding *bow numbers*. If such advertising is required, it shall be so stated in the Notice of Race. If advertising is for alcohol or tobacco, the word "may" instead of "shall" applies.

(ii) Sailboards

There shall be no reserved hull space on sailboards for event organizers.

The *organizing authority* of a sponsored event may permit or require the display of an advertisement of the event on both sides of the sail between the sail numbers and the wishbone (boom), on both sides of the sail aft of the foot median and on a bib worn by the competitors.

(e) competitors may display advertising on clothing and personal equipment without restriction.

20.3.2 In addition to 20.3.1, additional advertising chosen by the individual boat may be displayed in the following categories:

(a) Category A

No additional advertising.

(b) Category C

Advertising is permitted as per Category A, and in addition on hulls, spars and sails without restriction except the space reserved for identification by Appendix G and under section 20.3.1(b), (c) and (d).

20.3.3 When equipment is supplied by the event's *organizing authority*, Category C advertising on the supplied equipment is available to the *organizing authority*.

20.4 All Classes (except when participating in events listed in Regulation 20.6) - ISAF and Non-ISAF Status, National Classes

20.4.1 The right to choose Category A or C applies to all ISAF Classes, except Olympic Classes which shall be unrestricted Category C.

20.4.2 (a) The Class Associations of ISAF Classes may decide the advertising category to be applied to their class to be either A or C. If the Class Association makes no ruling, Category A shall apply.

(b) The Class Associations of Non-ISAF Classes (excluding *National Classes* referred to in Regulation 20.4.2(c) below) may decide the advertising category to be applied to their Class to be either A or C. If the Class Association makes no ruling, Category A shall apply.

(c) For *National Classes* the National Authority of the Class decides Category A or C. If the National Authority makes no ruling, Category A shall apply.

20.4.3 If Category C status is chosen, only the National Authority may introduce an Individual Advertising License System to permit its *competitors* to display advertising on their boats/sailboards. (A breach of a National Authority's license system is not protestable under this Code).

20.4.4 For *club or invitational events* the *organizing authority* may restrict advertising to Category A, with the approval of the National Authority of the organizing club. If Category C is decided, the ISAF Classes (except for Olympic Classes) and non-ISAF Classes (including *National Classes*) may decide the maximum level of advertising. Any restrictions within Category C shall be included in the Class Rules and subject to ISAF Council's approval. Olympic Classes cannot restrict Category C in anyway.

20.4.6 Except as provided by Regulations 20.3.1 and 20.3.3 the right to have any or all advertising on the hulls, sails and spars shall be solely the right of and at the direction of the *competitor* provided that such right may be contracted or assigned to others at the competitor's discretion.

20.5 *Handicapping Systems and Rating Rules*

20.5.1 The National Authority of a *competitor* in respect of the boat in which the competitor is competing, may decide the advertising category to be applied to boats racing under a handicap/measurement system to be either A or C. If Category C is decided, the said *competitor's* National Authority may decide the maximum level of advertising. If the National Authority makes no ruling, Category A shall apply.

Any "*Class*" (see definition of Class) or individual boat racing under a handicap/measurement system shall have its advertising category determined in accordance with the provisions of this clause.

20.5.2 For the purposes of Regulation 20.5.1, the provisions of Regulations 20.4.3, 20.4.4 and 20.4.6 shall apply.

20.6 *Special Events/Events of Classes/ISAF Events*

20.6.1 Category C applies.

20.6.2 ISAF will administer an Event Advertising System and/or Individual Advertising System for boats participating in the following events:

(i) Special Events
America's Cup Match and Challenger/Defender Series
Volvo Ocean Race
Global Ocean Races
Trans-Oceanic Races
ORC World Championships
Professional Windsurfers Association Events (PWA)

(ii) Events of Classes
International America's Cup Class
Volvo 60'
Maxi One Design
Open 60 Monohull Class (incorporates Open 50 Class)

Open 60 Multihull Class
PWA Classes
49'er Grand Prix series

(iii) Proposals for other Special Events and/or Events of Classes of equal or similar status may, on the initiative of the Executive Committee or on application by an event *organizing authority* (with the approval of the relevant National Authority) to the Executive Committee and with its consent, be made to the Council for its approval.

(iv) ISAF Events
ISAF World Youth Sailing Championship
ISAF Combined Olympic Classes World Championship
ISAF World Sailing Championship
ISAF Match Racing World Championship
ISAF Women's World Match Racing Championship
ISAF Team Racing World Championship
ISAF Women's Keelboat World Championship

And any other ISAF Events which may be introduced.

20.7 *Fees*
20.7.1 All boats carrying Category C advertising in line with Regulations 20.4 and 20.5 may be required to pay a fee only to their National Authority (no share to ISAF or any other National Authorities).

20.7.2 All Events under Regulation 20.6 carrying Category C advertising shall pay a fee to ISAF (no share to any National Authority).

[Note: Sections 20.7.1 and 20.7.2 to be reviewed after 2 years (November 2003), before a final decision on the distribution of fees is decided].

20.8 Entry Fees
There should be no variation of entry fees based on the *competitor's* category of advertising for the boat in which he is competing.

20.9 *Protests under this Code*
20.9.1 When, after finding the facts, a protest committee decides that a boat or her crew has broken a section of this Code, it shall:

(a) give a warning; or

(b) disqualify the boat in accordance with RRS 64.1; or

(c) disqualify the boat from more than one race or from the series when it decides that the breach warrants a stronger penalty; or

(d) act under RRS 69.1 when it decides that there may have been a gross breach.

20. 10 *Definitions*
The following definitions shall apply to this Code only:

Note: There are some definitions which are not needed in the present text of the Code.

(a) "All Classes"
Shall include all Classes as defined below and shall include Classes which are designated as ISAF Classes as well as Classes which are not designated as ISAF Classes.

(b) "Class"
A Class of boat/sailboard includes boats/sailboards which conform to a physical specification intended to allow competitive racing among the Class, and without limiting the generality of the foregoing, includes Classes with one-design, restricted, and developmental specifications as these terms are applied generally and for which there is an existing organization to administer the Class which has:

(i) an Executive or similar body which administers the Class,

(ii) a membership which is open to all owners of boats/sailboards which meet the specification of the Class, and

(iii) which holds a meeting of members at least once a year, and which gives notice of such meetings to all members.

(c) "National Class"
A National Class for the purposes of this Regulation is a class where the National Authority has substantial authority in the direction or management of the Class.

(d) "Club or Invitational Event"
A Club event is an event that is sponsored, organized or held by a Club which has sailing as one of its activities. An Invitational event is one in which the participants are invited and is not open to members of a participating class except by invitation.

A yacht club hosting an event which is a qualifier in any way for an International Class event cannot declare an Event Category "A" by making the event an "invitational".

(e) "Hull Length"
For the purposes of this Regulation, Hull Length is as defined in the applicable Class rules for Hull Length or any comparable measurement less Hull Appendages and if no means of measurement exists in the Class rules, Hull Length and Hull Appendage shall have the meaning set out in the Equipment Rules of Sailing, D.3.1 and E.1.1.

(f) "Organizing Authority"
Shall have the definition contained in RRS 87.1.

(g) "Competitor"
In addition to its natural meaning, a competitor in respect of any boat shall include any person who has the right to use the boat as owner or by charter, loan or otherwise.

(h) "Competitor Advertising"
In respect of any boat is advertising which is applied to a boat, its equipment or the person or the equipment of a competitor or competitors as the condition of or as the result of a payment made to or made as a result of the direction of one or more of the competitors in respect of such boat.

(i) "Other Advertising"
Advertising which is not competitor advertising.

(j) "Bow Number"
An identifier assigned to a boat, usually for the duration of an event, by the organizer which is required to be displayed on the bow of a boat which may be a combination of numbers and letters.

NOTE: Regulation 20 is subject to change by the ISAF Council. The current text of the regulation is available from the ISAF by mail, fax or e-mail (sail@isaf.co.uk).

APPENDIX 2 – ISAF ELIGIBILITY CODE

See rule 75.2. This appendix shall not be changed by sailing instructions or prescriptions of national authorities.

REGULATION 21
21. ISAF ELIGIBILITY CODE
21.1 *ISAF Eligibility Rules*
To be eligible to compete in an event listed in rule 21.2.1, a competitor shall:

(a) be governed by the regulations and rules of the ISAF;

(b) be a member of a Member National Authority or one of its affiliated organizations. Such membership shall be established by the competitor

(i) being entered by the national authority of the country of which the competitor is a national or ordinarily a resident; or

(ii) presenting a valid membership card or certificate, or other satisfactory evidence of identity and membership;

(c) not be under suspension of ISAF eligibility.

21.2 Events Requiring ISAF Eligibility
21.2.1 ISAF eligibility is required for the following events:

(a) the sailing regatta of the Olympic Games;

(b) the sailing regattas of regional games recognised by the International Olympic Committee;

(c) events including 'ISAF' in their titles;

(d) world and continental championships of ISAF international classes and of the Offshore Racing Council;
(e) any other event approved by the ISAF as a world championship and so stated in the notice of race and the sailing instructions;

(f) any event approved by a national authority or the ISAF as an

Olympic qualifying event;

(g) all other international events involving an ISAF International Judge, Umpire, Race Officer or Measurer. For the purposes of this rule, international events are ISAF events, world and continental championships, and events described as international events in their notices of race and sailing instructions; and

(h) all events using the Racing Rules of Sailing.

21.2.2 ISAF eligibility may be required for any other event when so stated in the notice of race and the sailing instructions with specific reference to this regulation.

21.3 *Suspension of ISAF Eligibility*

21.3.1 After proper inquiry by either the national authority of the competitor or the ISAF Executive Committee, a competitor's ISAF eligibility shall be promptly suspended with immediate effect, permanently or for a specified period of time

(a) for any suspension of eligibility in accordance with RRS 69.2; or

(b) for breaking RRS 5; or

(c) for competing, within the two years preceding the inquiry, in an event that the competitor knew or should have known was a prohibited event.

21.3.2 A prohibited event is an event:

(a) permitting or requiring advertising beyond that permitted by the ISAF Advertising Code;

(b) with prizes or other benefits referred to in Regulation 8.2 that is a national event not approved by the national authority of the venue or an international event not approved by the ISAF;

(c) that is described as a world championship or uses the word "world", either in the title of the event or otherwise, and that is not approved by the ISAF; or

(d) that does not conform to the requirements of RRS 87, and is not otherwise approved by the ISAF.

21.3.3 When an event described in rule 21.3.2 has been approved as required, that fact shall be stated in the notice of race and the sailing instructions.

21.4 *Reports; Reviews; Notification; Appeals*

21.4.1 When a national authority suspends a competitor's ISAF eligibility under rule 21.3.1, it shall promptly report the suspension and reasons therefor to the ISAF. The ISAF Executive Committee may revise or annul the suspension with immediate effect. The ISAF shall promptly report any suspension of a competitor's eligibility, or of its revision or annulment by the ISAF Executive Committee, to all national authorities, international class associations, the Offshore Racing Council and other ISAF affiliated organizations, which may also suspend eligibility for events held within their jurisdiction.

21.4.2 A competitor whose suspension of ISAF eligibility has been either imposed by a national authority, or imposed or revised by the ISAF Executive Committee, shall be advised of the right to appeal to the ISAF Review Board and be provided with a copy of the Review Board Rules of Procedure.

21.4.3 A national authority or the ISAF Executive Committee may ask for a review of its decision by the ISAF Review Board by complying with the Review Board Rules of Procedure.

21.4.4 The Review Board Rules of Procedure shall govern all appeals and requests for review.

21.4.5 Upon an appeal or request for review, the ISAF Review Board may confirm, revise or annul a suspension of eligibility, or require a hearing or rehearing by the suspending authority.

21.4.6 Decisions of the Review Board are not subject to appeal.

21.4.7 The ISAF shall promptly notify all national authorities, international class associations and the Offshore Racing Council of all Review Board decisions.

NOTE: Regulation 21 is subject to change by the ISAF Council. The current text of the regulation is available from the ISAF by mail, fax or e-mail (sail@isaf.co.uk).

APPENDIX 3 – ISAF ANTI-DOPING CODE

See rule 5. This appendix shall not be changed by sailing instructions or prescriptions of national authorities.

REGULATION 19
19.ISAF ANTI-DOPING CODE
The doping definition of the ISAF Medical Commission, like that of the International Olympic Committee (IOC), is based on the banning of pharmacological classes of agents.

The definition has the advantage that also new drugs, some of which may be especially designed for doping purposes, are prohibited.

The list published in Appendix "A" of Olympic Movement Anti-Doping Code (OMADC) - and detailed at the end of Regulation 19 - represents examples of the different dope classes to illustrate the doping definition. Unless indicated, all substances belonging to the banned classes may not be used for medical treatment, even if they are not listed as examples. If substances of the banned classes are detected in the IOC accredited laboratory, the ISAF Medical Commission will report to the ISAF Executive Committee who will act upon the advice of the ISAF Anti-Doping Panel.

The presence of the drug in a sample of urine or blood constitutes an offence, irrespective of the route of administration.

Doping Controls shall be undertaken in the sport of sailing.

When governmental requirements conflict with parts of this ISAF Anti-Doping Code those requirements apply.

The following are basic ISAF requirements:

Procedures

19.1 *Selection of Competitors*

19.1.1 A reasonable number of doping control tests, both in-competition (ICT) and out-of-competition (OOCT), shall be undertaken.

19.1.2 In-competition is defined as that period of time between the scheduled time of the warning signal of the first race of the event, up to the closure of *protest* time following the final race of the event.

19.1.3 Out-of-competition testing is defined as testing which takes place at other times outside the ICT period. When a doping control is conducted on the day of a competition in which the affected competitor has competed or is entered or expected to compete, the test shall be considered as in-competition. All other unannounced doping control shall be deemed to be OOCT. OOCT may be conducted by ISAF, by an ISAF authorized organisation or on behalf and in collaboration with the World Anti-Doping Agency (WADA) or by WADA authorized organisation at any time, or a recognised governmental agency, including at the time or location of any competition in every member country. Preferably it shall be carried out without any advance notice to the competitor or his/her Member National Authority (MNA).

19.1.4 ISAF and/or WADA may keep a register of competitors who are being subject to OOCT. Member National Authorities have the obligation to submit names, current places of living, addresses, telephone numbers, training times and training and competition locations for individuals and teams requested by ISAF and WADA, to enable ISAF and WADA to conduct OOCT.

19.1.5 ISAF and/or WADA can select competitors being subject to OOCT among all Member National Authority competitors. The selection can be done by ballot or any other principle that is decided by ISAF and/or WADA.

19.1.6 A competitor selected for sample taking shall not refuse to have a sample taken either in or out-of-competition, when required to do so by an accredited sampling officer acting on behalf of a Member National Authority, ISAF, WADA, IOC or a recognised governmental agency.

19.1.7 Doping Control is administered in order to uphold the requirements of RRS Fundamental Rule 5.

19.1.8 At an authorized event where doping control is undertaken, the protest committee chairman shall select competitors to be sampled on a specific day. Selection may be by means of a draw and specific competitors may be selected, as decided by the protest committee chairman. If on that day a race is postponed to a following day or abandoned, or if a competitor does not start in a race that is taking place, the protest committee chairman may still require the sampling of the specific competitor(s) already selected and may select any other competitors to be tested on that day. When there is more than one competitor in each boat, any or all of them may be selected. The race committee shall give to the sampling officer the names of the competitors selected for sampling. A competitor may be sampled more than once during an event.

19.2 *Sample Taking*
19.2.1 (a) The accredited sampling officer or his/her representative shall inform a competitor by written notice, which shall be given to the competitor, in confidence, that he or she has been selected for sample taking and is required to provide a urine or a blood sample at the time and place specified in the notice. The notice shall specify the name of the sampling officer appointed for the event (or OOCT) and of the designated laboratory (IOC accredited) to which the specimens will be sent.

(b) The competitor shall, during in-competition testing, sign an undertaking to be present at the Doping Control Station by a specific time, which will usually be not later than one hour after the time of notification. In back to back racing a competitor shall be notified at the conclusion of the race from which he/she has been selected, and extra time shall be allowed for the competitor to take part in any subsequent races that day, before returning to shore for Doping Control.

After notifying the competitor the organizing committee representative for doping control should remain with the competitor at all times (unless racing) until they together arrive at the Doping Control Station.

(c) The competitor may be accompanied by one person of his or her choice.

(d) A competitor who fails to appear at the appointed time and place, or who refuses to provide a sample shall be disqualified and sanctioned, together with the boat in which he or she was sailing, from the event and all the results to date shall be expunged. The protest committee shall call a hearing in accordance with RRS Part 5 Section B, to investigate the circumstances, to consider reasons offered to explain the failure to provide a sample in proper time, and report its findings to the initiating national authority, and to the national authority of the competitor.

19.2.2 The protocol for sample taking procedures at Doping Controls is detailed in Appendix "C" of the OMADC.

19.2.3 The competitor and the accompanying person shall be attended in the waiting room of the Doping Control Centre by a member of the doping control team.

19.2.4 The member of the doping control team shall check the identity of the competitor and his/her sail number.

19.2.5 The time of arrival and personal data of the competitor shall be recorded.

19.2.6 Wherever possible only one competitor plus attendant/team official at a time should be called into the Doping Control Office. Where several tests are taking place this may not be possible.

19.2.7 In addition to the competitor and accompanying person only the following may be present in the Doping Control Office:
- A representative from ISAF;
- A member of the ISAF Medical Commission or their nominee;
- The officials in charge of taking samples and keeping records;
- An interpreter if required.

Photographs may not be taken in the Doping Control Station during the doping control procedure, unless required by the Doping Control Official in charge of the Doping Control Station. Representatives of the press are not allowed to be present during testing.

19.2.8 (a) When a competitor has been selected for OOCT the Sampling Officer (SO) appointed by ISAF or International Doping Control Officer (IDCO) appointed by WADA may either make an appointment to meet the competitor or, at preference, he/she may arrive unannounced at the competitor's training camp, accommodation or any other place where the competitor is likely to be found. In either case, the SO/IDCO shall provide proof of identity and provide a letter of appointment from

ISAF or WADA. The SO/IDCO shall also require proof of identity of the competitor. The actual collection of the sample shall be in as much accordance with OMADC and Regulation 19 as is reasonable.

(b) Arrangements for collection of the sample shall be made as soon as possible after the appointment with the competitor has been made. It is the competitor's responsibility to check the arranged date, time and the precise location of the meeting.

(c) Where the SO/IDCO arrives unannounced he/she must give the competitor reasonable time to complete activity in which he/she is engaged, but testing should commence as soon as possible.

(d) In case a Team Doctor is not available or present at the OOCT, the competitor is responsible for declaring all medication taken by him/her in the 72 hours prior to the sample collection time. The Team Doctor does not need to be present to give written details or declare medication that the competitor is subject to. It is understood that the OOCT sample procedure is fully valid without the presence and without the declaration on the report form from the Team Doctor.

(e) Each competitor selected for OOCT shall, as part of the collection procedure, in conjunction with the SO/IDCO complete such laboratory forms as are required by the initiating authority or laboratory to whom the sample is to be dispatched.

(f) If the competitor refuses to provide a urine sample, the SO/IDCO shall note this on the doping control form used, enter his name on the form and ask the competitor to sign the form. The SO/IDCO shall also note any other irregularities in the doping control process.

(g) The nature of unannounced OOCT makes it desirable that little or no prior warning is given to the competitor. Every effort will be made by the SO/IDCO to collect the sample speedily and efficiently with the minimum of interruption to the competitor's training, social or work arrangements. If there is interruption, however, no competitor may take any action to gain compensation for any inconvenience incurred.

(h) If OOCT are conducted by WADA or by a WADA authorized organisation, the original copy of the doping control form will be sent to ISAF and a copy will be kept in the possession of WADA.

(i) ISAF shall nominate a contact person responsible for the OOCT Testing liaison with WADA

(j) There has been signed an agreement between WADA and ISAF, the articles, terms and conditions of which are on record at ISAF. Under this agreement WADA will conduct OOCT services on behalf of ISAF in accordance with the OMADC and Regulation 19.

19.2.9 In ICT and OOCT the sampling procedure shall be carefully explained to the competitor in his/her own language or with the aid of an interpreter. It shall be made clear to the competitor that the sampling officer who directly supervises the passing of the urine sample shall be of the same sex as the competitor.

19.2.10 If the competitor refuses to provide a sample the possible consequences shall be explained to the competitor. If the competitor still refuses, this fact shall be noted in the records. These shall be signed by the official in charge of the station, the technician, representatives of the national authority which organized the sampling, and of any representative of ISAF who may be present and may be signed by the competitor and accompanying person. Following investigation the Member National Authority shall report findings and decisions relating to sanctions applied, to ISAF.

19.2.11 (a) The appropriately provided urine sample will be divided by the competitor into two samples "A" and "B" and placed in individual bottles which are sealed into individual containers. Codes shall identify the bottles and containers such that the laboratory does not know the name of any competitor.

(b) Samples collected during testing shall be forwarded in the appropriate sealed containers to the designated, IOC accredited, laboratory concerned. The sample taking, transportation and analysis shall be as detailed in Appendix "C" of the OMADC. During transportation to the laboratory a record of the chain of custody shall be made from the time of production of the sample by the competitor to the time of opening of a container in the laboratory. At all times following its collection the sample shall be stored in the conditions required by the laboratory.

19.2.12 The analysis of sample "A" shall be conducted by the

accredited laboratory, and the result made available to the initiating authority, within 30 days of the taking of the sample at the Doping Control Centre.

19.2.13 The competitor shall provide a postal, fax or e-mail address at which during the 60 days following the taking of the sample required, he or she may be informed of the laboratory analysis results of sample "A". Should sample "A" provide a positive result the address given will be used to inform the competitor, and to invite the competitor to attend or to be represented at the laboratory during the subsequent analysis of the "B" sample. Sample "B" shall be analysed within 10 days of the date of notification of the "A" sample result.

Failure by a competitor to acknowledge receipt of the notice requiring his/her presence for the provision of a sample, or to sign the doping control form, or to provide a contact address will not be grounds for cancelling any penalty imposed for breaking RRS Fundamental Rule 5.

19.3 *Sample Analysis*
19.3.1 The Laboratory Analysis Procedures shall follow the protocol detailed in Appendix "D" of the OMADC.

19.3.2 Analysis shall only be carried out in laboratories accredited by the IOC. Such laboratories are listed as Appendix "C" to the OMADC and shall be regularly inspected to maintain accreditation standards.

19.3.3 Sample "A" is analysed first. If sample "A" is negative, ie. no proscribed medication or its metabolites are present, or no abnormal ratios or quantities for the presence of certain substances by the OMADC are noted, no further action is taken.

19.3.4 When "A" sample is positive, ie. proscribed medication, metabolites or abnormal substance levels are noted:

(a) the initiating authority shall so inform the competitor and his/her national authority immediately. No race results shall be changed at this stage; and

(b) the laboratory will proceed to test sample "B", the competitor or his/her representative may be present at the testing, and shall be informed of its time and place.

(c) when sample "B" is negative, the initiating authority shall so inform the competitor and his/her national authority, no further action shall be taken.

(d) when no result has been obtained from sample "B" after 60 days from the date of the sample taking, the procedure shall be considered void and no further action shall be taken.

(e) when sample "B" is positive the initiating national authority, or ISAF in testing initiated by ISAF, will inform the competitor in writing at the address provided (see Regulation 19.2.13) and his/her national authority.

(f) any penalties imposed by the national authority against a competitor/participant who is found in breach of RRS Fundamental Rule 5, or of Regulation 19 shall be reported promptly to ISAF.

19.3.5 Sanctions shall be applied in the first instance by the Member National Authority, which shall inform ISAF of its decisions. If the Member National Authority imposes no penalty, or an inadequate penalty, the possibility of imposing sanctions may be reviewed by ISAF.

19.4 *Penalties*

19.4.1 The penalties for doping are stated in the OMADC.

19.4.2 In addition to any penalty imposed under Regulation 21.3 a competitor who has found in breach of RRS Fundamental Rule 5 shall have his/her ISAF Eligibility suspended as provided in Regulation 21 - Eligibility Code.

19.4.3 The competitor may appeal as provided in Regulation 21 and as Regulation 19.5.5 below.

19.5 *Hearings and Appeals Procedure*
19.5.1 The competitor has 20 days from the date of the communication required by Regulation 19.3.4(e) to request a hearing or appeal to his/her Member National Authority, or to ISAF if the testing was initiated by ISAF.

19.5.2 If no appeal has been lodged after the last day for any such appeal has passed, one or more of the penalties provided for in

Regulation 19.4 will be applied with effect from the event during which the relevant testing took place and any subsequent event prior to the testing of the "B" sample and during 20 days thereafter.

19.5.3 The findings of positive results shall be reported to ISAF, together with details of sanctions applied by the Member National Authority.

19.5.4 Competitors who have positive doping control results and who appeal against the finding of a breach of any of the anti-doping codes to which the competitor is subject or against the sanctions applied may be referred to the ISAF Anti-Doping Panel. The Anti-Doping Panel will consider evidence and report to the ISAF Executive Committee. The participant appealing is entitled to a copy of such procedures at the time he/she is notified of a positive result pursuant to Regulation 19.3.4(e).

19.5.5 Since ISAF recognises the Court of Arbitration for Sport a participant may appeal the decision of the ISAF Executive Committee to the Court of Arbitration for Sport in accordance with the provisions for appeal of the Court. A copy of those provisions shall be provided to the participant at the time he/she is notified of the Panel's decision.

19.6 *Exemptions*
19.6.1 A competitor may request, only in writing, prior approval from the ISAF Medical Commission for the use of a banned substance, or a banned method, for special medical reasons. The reasons to be supported by written evidence from a specialist doctor. For the Olympic Games, dispensation can only be granted by the IOC Medical Commission, via an appeal made by the ISAF Medical Commission, the request to be made on behalf of the competitor, to ISAF, by his/her Member National Authority.

19.6.2 In Offshore races of more than 50 nautical miles, the use during a race of any banned substance or banned procedure for emergency medical treatment shall be reported promptly to the protest committee, which shall inform the appropriate national authority and the ISAF. The ISAF Medical Commission may retroactively approve such use.

19.7 *Expenses*
19.7.1 Any expenses in travel to observe analysis of a "B" sample, or to give evidence on his/her own behalf, incurred in connection with this ISAF Anti-Doping Code by a competitor shall be his or her responsibility and neither the participant's National Authority or ISAF shall have any obligation for any such expenses.

19.8 *Team Doctors*
19.8.1 With the approval of ISAF or a Member National Authority or National Olympic Committee (NOC), a Team Doctor or a Doctor who is responsible for sailing competitors, officials and others in the care of that Doctor, may carry and employ such medications as the circumstances may require, and as might be expected to be properly used in the undertaking of the Hippocratic oath.

19.9 *Team Disqualification*
19.9.1 In the event that a competitor who is a member of a team is found guilty of doping, the boat upon which the offending sailor was a crew member shall be disqualified from the event. In sailing events in which more than one boat represents an individual national or other team, the boat upon which the offending sailor was a crew member shall be disqualified, but not other boats within a group of boats sailing as a team in either one or a number of classes.

19.10 *Declaration of Medications*
19.10.1 The use of the proscribed beta-2 agonists, which are classified as stimulants, is permitted, by inhalation only, in cases of proven asthma. They are permitted following written request, prior to an event, by the competitor to the relevant medical authority. The relevant doctor shall issue a certificate granting permission for the inhaler(s) to be used, and shall maintain a record of the issue of the certificate.

The relevant medical officer shall preferably be the Member National Authority doctor. In the event of the Member National Authority having no doctor appointed the request should be made to the ISAF Medical Commission.

Diabetics requiring insulin are also required to notify the relevant medical authority to obtain a certificate.

Notification Procedure
1. Competitors requiring treatment involving permitted beta-2 agonists by inhalation, or insulin, should note details of the treatment in writing, including diagnosis and the name and address of the prescribing physician.
2. A copy of this information is sent in confidence to the Member

National Authority Medical Officer, or in his absence to the ISAF Medical Commission.
3. The Member National Authority Medical Officer may wish to seek further information from the competitor or physician.
4. If diagnosis and treatment are accepted, the Member National Authority Medical Officer will send a certificate agreeing to the medication to the competitor, and maintain a record at the Member National Authority.
5. Further notification may be required, at intervals, for long term treatment.

19.11 *Dispensation for taking Proscribed Medication*
19.11.1 If dispensation is requested for medication other than that listed in Regulation 19.10 above the Member National Authority Medical Officer will be required to request full medical details from the competitor, including diagnosis, names of specialists consulted, their address, hospital letters etc. These should be sent in confidence to the Chairman ISAF Medical Commission, with a request, backed by the Member National Authority, that dispensation for the taking of the listed medications be granted.

Following investigation such a dispensation may be granted by the ISAF Executive Committee for a fixed period subject to review. This will enable the sailor to compete in events held under ISAF rules.

19.11.2 For the Olympic Regatta dispensation can only be granted by the IOC, acting upon the advice of the IOC Medical Commission. To obtain this dispensation the Member National Authority should apply to the ISAF Medical Commission. The Member National Authority will be requested to provide full details as outlined above. The ISAF Medical Commission will then, if they agree to the request, submit a documented application to the IOC Medical Commission.

19.11.3 An ISAF Dispensation alone does not permit the sailor to compete in the Olympic Regatta.

19.12 *Classes of Prohibited Substances in Certain Circumstances*
19.12.1 Where in the OMADC in Appendix "A" under III provides an option in the adoption of any substance on the proscribed list of medication, this choice of adoption will be made by the ISAF Executive Committee upon the advice of the Medical Commission.

19.12.2 Pursuant to Regulation 19.12.1:
- Beta Blockers are permitted in sailing except for Match Race Helms .

19.13 *ISAF Anti-Doping Panel*

19.13.1 The ISAF Anti-Doping Panel will consist of:
- Executive Committee member - Chair
- Chairman, or alternative appointed by Chairman, of Medical Commission,
- Chairman, or alternative appointed by Chairman, of Racing Rules Committee,
- Chairman, or alternative appointed by Chairman, of Constitution Committee.
and may be called upon to consider breaches of the OMADC and Regulation 19 and then report to the ISAF Executive Committee.

NOTE: Regulation 19 is subject to change by the ISAF Council. The current text of the regulation is available from the ISAF by mail, fax or e-mail (sail@isaf.co.uk).

The Olympic Movement Anti-Doping Code, Appendix A (IOC Prohibited Classes of Substances and Prohibited Methods), List of Examples of Prohibited Substances and Prohibited Methods, and other current information about the Code are also available on the ISAF website.

INDEX

Index entries contain references to rule numbers, appendices, and sections of the rule book (for example, Introduction, Race Signals). Italics indicate defined words. Defined words whose text includes a primary index word appear in italics at the end of the primary word entry. Appendices J, K, 1, 2 and 3 are not indexed in detail.

Abandon: Race Signals, 27.3, 32, 35, 64.2, C3.2(d)(e), E3.10, N3, *postpone*, *racing*
acceptance of the rules: 3
advantage gained by breaking rule: 44.1, C8.3(a), D2.2(d), D3.1(b)
advantage gained by touching *mark*: 31.2
advertising: Introduction, 76.1, 79, B7.2, J.1.2(1), J2.2(1), Appendix 1
aground: 21, 42.3(d), E4.2(b)
allegations of gross misconduct (See gross misconduct)
anchor, anchored, anchoring: 21, 45
anchor line of *mark*: 18.1(a), 19.2, *mark*
Anti-Doping Code, ISAF: Introduction, Appendix 3
appeal (measurement), intent to, and further competition: 64.3(c)
appeal, comments on to national authority: F6
appeal, no right of: 70.4, C9.1, D2.2(h)
appeal, right of: 3(b), 70
appeal, withdrawing: F7
appeal decisions: 71
appeal of international jury decision: M1.7
appeal procedures: 3(b), 70.5, F preamble, F1–F7, L6
arm signals: C2.7
attention signal: C3.2(d)(e)
avoid(ing) contact: 14, 18.3(a)

Backing a sail: 20, B2.1
bail out: 45
ballast: 51, E4.7(a)
banned substances, methods: 5, Appendix 3
beat to windward: 17.2, 18.1(b), 42.3(b), D1.1(a)
Black Flag rule (30.3), black flag: Race Signals, 26, 27.2, 30.3, 36, 63.1, 80, 88.3(b), A5, A11, C5(d), D2.2(e) E3.6
boat owner: 2, 3, 69.1(c), 69.2(c), 78.1, E6, G1.1(c)
Bonus Point System, scoring: 88.3, A4
boom: 50.3, C7.3(a)
bowsprit: 50.3(a)
breach of, breaking a rule: Sportsmanship and the Rules, 5, 36, 44.1, 60.1, 63.3(a), 64.1, 68, 69.1(a), 69.2(a), 88.3(b), C6.6(b), C8.3(c), D2.2(d), D3.1(b), D5.3, E5.1, E5.7, L5.3
breakdowns: D5

Capsize, capsized: 21, B1, B2.2, D5.3, E2
centreboard adjustment for propulsion: 42.2(b)
certificate (See measurement, rating certificate)
change, changing course: 16, 18.2(d), 19, *keep clear*, *obstruction*
change of course by race committee: Race Signals, 33
changes to rules (See rules, changes to)
changes to sailing instructions (See sailing instructions, changes to)
changing trim or stability: 51
class, international: 76.2, G1
class association: 76.2, 87.1(d), G1.1(c), G2
class flag: Race Signals, 26
class insignia: 77, B7, G1.1(a), G1.3, G2

class rules: Introduction, *rule*
class rules, changes to, in sailing instructions: J2.2(7)
class rules, clothing and equipment: 43.1(b)
class rules, complying with: 78
class rules, measurement *protests*: 64.3(a)
class rules, sail identification: G
class rules and *racing* rule changes: Introduction, 86.1(c), G5
clear ahead, *clear astern*: 12, 17.1, 17.2, 18.2(b)(c), 18.5, C2.3, C2.6
close-hauled boat: 19.1
close-hauled course: 13, 18.3(a), C7.2(a), C7.3(a)
clothing and equipment: 43, H
collision: 41, 42.3(d)
conduct of a race: 25–36, 85, 88.1, B3, E3, M2.3(b)
conflicting rules (See rules, conflicting)
contact: 14, D1.2(a), E3.1, *keep clear*
costs, measurement *protest*: 64.3(d)
course, changing: 16, 18.2(d), 19.1, C2.11, D1.1(d), *keep clear*, *obstruction*
course, proper (See *proper course*)
course, sailing the: 28, 32.1, 35
course board: E3.2
course change by race committee: Race Signals, 32, 33, E3.10
crew and movement of body: 42.2, 42.3
crew at *finish*, *start*: 29.1, 30, C2.1, C3.2
crew position: 49

Damage: 14(b), 62.1(b), C6, D1.2(b), D2, D3.1(b), E5.9
damage, serious: 44.1, 60.4, 63.5
damages, financial: 68
danger: 1.1, 21, 42.3(c), 47.2
decision to race: 4
diagram of incident: 65.2, F2.2, L3.3
disciplinary action: 62.1(d), 69.2(a)
disqualification, measurement: 64.3(c)
disqualification and scoring: 2, 67, A4.2, A6, A9, A11, C5(d), C7.2(f), C8.5, C10.4(b)
disqualification of *party* to a protest: 64.1(a)
disqualification without hearing: 30.3, 67, N2.1, N2.3
downwind: C2.4, C7.2(a), *leeward* and *windward*
drugs, banned substances: 5, Appendix 3
dry suit: 40

Eligibility, suspension of, questions: 69.2, 69.3, M2.2(a), Appendix 2
Eligibility Code, ISAF: Introduction, Appendix 2
English, use of, in prescriptions: 88.2(b)
entry, qualification to race: 75–80
equipment: 1.2, 43, D5.3, E4.5(c), M2.2, *clear astern* and clear ahead, finish, start
equipment and class rules: 78.3
equipment and crew limitations: 47
Equipment Rules of Sailing:J1.1(3), J2.1(2)
equipment weighing: 43, H1, H3

error by race committee, *protest* committee: 29.3, 32.1(a), 62.1(a), 66
error in starting, sailing course: 20, 28.1, 29.2, 32.1(a), *finish*
evidence: 63.3(a), 63.5, 63.6, 64.2, 69.1(d), L3.2
evidence, new and significant: 66, F5, L3.1, L4
excluded scores (See scoring and excluded races)
exclusion of boat or competitor: 69.1(b), 76, C6.6(c), E5.8(a)
exoneration: 64.1(b), C8.1(b), E5.8

Facts found: 63.6, 65.1, 70.1, 71.3, E5.7, F5, L3.3, M1.4(b)
fair play: 2
fair sailing: 2
fairness of competition: 32.1(e), M2.1
fairness of redress decision: 64.2
finish: Race Signals, 28.1, 31, A3, C2.1, D1.1(c), D3.2, E1.1, *proper course*, *racing*
finishing line: Race Signals, 28.1, 44.3, C3.3, D2.1(b), E3.7, finish, *mark*, *racing*
finishing mark: Race Signals, 31.1, 31.2, *racing*
finishing times, adjustment: 64.2
flags (See Race Signals, *starting signals*, Black Flag rule, red flag)
floorboards: 51
fog signals: 48
footwear: 43.1(b)
forestays and headsail *tacks*: 54
four-length zone: E1.3

General recall (See recall)
government rules: Part 2 preamble, 48, J2.2(3)
gross misconduct rule (See misconduct)
gybe, gybing: 17.2, 18 preamble, 18.4, 42.2(e), 42.3(a), 50.2, D1.1(a)

Hail, come within: Race Signals
hail, out of radio control: E4.9
hail and arm signal: C2.7
hail and time to respond: 19.1
hail by race, *protest* committee: E3.8, E3.9, N1
hail for room:19.1
hail in *protesting*: 61.1(a), D2.1(a), D2.2, E3.1, E5.2, L3.1
hailing distance, beyond: 61.1(a)
harness: 43.1(b)
hauling out: 45
head to wind: 13, 18.2(c), C7.3(a), *leeward* and *windward*
headsail: 50, 54, G1.1
hearing, correcting details at: 61.2
hearing, dissatisfaction with jury panel: M1.4(b)
hearing, not entitled to: D2.2(a)
hearing, penalty without: 30.2, 30.3, 63.1, 67, A5, N2
hearing, reopening: 63.3(b), 66, 71.2, C9.1, D2.2(h), E5.10, F5, L4
hearing, right to be present: 63.3, E5.6
hearing, umpired races: D2.2(f)
hearings and decisions: 61.1(c), 63–68, 71.2, C6.6, L3.4 (See also redress)
hearing and rule 42: 67
hearing and rule 69: 69
hearing procedures, requirements for, recommendations: 63.1, F5, L, *party*

hiking harness, straps: 43.1(b), 49.1
hiking straps: 49.1
hull appendages: 52
hull lengths, within two: 17.1, 17.2, 61.1(a), C7.3(a), D1.1(a), *two-length zone*

Identification on sails: 77, B7, E6, G
illness, injury: 41, 47.2, 60.4, 63.5, M1.5
in writing, appeal decision: 71.4
in writing, gross misconduct allegation: 69.1(a)
in writing, measurement issues, 43.1(c), 64.3(c), 78.3
in writing, *protest*, *protest* decisions: 61.2, 65.2, D2.2(g)
in writing, redress request: 62.2, E5.5(b)
in writing, sailing instructions changes: 88.2(a)
individual recall (See recall)
informing competitor, rule 42 disqualification: 67
informing competitor, rule 69 hearing: 69.1(a)
informing national authorities: 69.3, L5.5
informing parties to a hearing: 65, F4, L1, L3.5
informing *protest* committee: C8.4
informing protestee: 61.1, E5.2
informing race committee, scoring penalty: 44.3(a)
informing umpires: C6.4(b)
injury, serious: 60.4, 63.5
inside boat: 18 preamble, 18.2
inside *overlap*: 18.4, 18.5
interested party: 60.2(a), 60.3(a), 63.4, E1.3, M3.3, L2
interfere, interfering: 22, C2.9, C2.10, C9.2, D1.1(c), D2.2(h)
international class: 76.2, G1
international event: 88.2(b)
International Judge: 70.4(c), M1.2, M1.4
international jury, appeal of decisions: 70.4, M1.7
international jury, composition, appointment, organization, procedures, responsibilities: 70.4(c), 87.2, 89(c), M1, M2
international jury panel: M3.4
International Regulations for Preventing Collisions at Sea: Part 2 preamble, 48, J2.2(3)
International Sailing Federation (See ISAF)
interpretation of rule, request for: 70.3, F2.3
ISAF: Introduction
ISAF Advertising Code: Introduction, Appendix 1
ISAF Anti-Doping Code: Introduction, Appendix 3
ISAF Council: Appendices Section II preamble
ISAF Eligibility Code: Introduction, Appendix 2
ISAF Executive Committee: 69.3
ISAF regulations: Introduction, 5, 87.2, 89(c), Appendices Section II preamble

Jury: 87.2, 89(b), M (See also international jury)

Keep clear: Part 2 Section A preamble, 10–17, 18.2, 18.5, 20, 62.1(b), C2.8, E5.5(a), *obstruction*
knockout series: C10.5, C11.2, C11.3

Leeward and *windward*: 11, 17.1, 17.2, C7.2(a), C7.4(a), D1.1(a), *keep clear*
life-jacket (personal buoyancy): Race Signals, 1.2, 27.1, 40, E1.4
lifelines: 49.2
life-saving equipment: 1.2
line (See finishing line, starting line)
Low Point System, scoring: 88.3, A4

Mainsail: 50.1, *leeward and windward*
manual power: 52
mark: finish, *two-length zone, racing*
mark, approaching, fetching, tacking, gybing at: 18.3, 18.4
mark, missing or out of position: Race Signals, 32.1(d), 34
mark, required side and correct order: 28
mark, rounding, passing: 18.1, 18.2, 28.1, C7.2(c)
mark, starting: 27.2, 28.2, 31.1, C4.1
mark, touching, holding: 31, 44.4(a), B3
mark and change of course signal: 33
mark and penalty: 31.2, C7.3(b)
match *racing* rules: C
measurement, rating certificates: 78, B5, M2.2(a)
measurement *protests*, decisions: 64.3, 65.3, 78.3
measurement *rule*, doubt about: 64.3(b)
measurer and class *rules*: 78.3
misconduct, gross: 36, 60.2(c), 62.1(d), 69, 86.1(a), D2.2(f), L5, N2.3, *party*
moorings: 45
movable ballast: 51, E4.7
moving astern: 20, B2.1

National authority: Introduction, 66, 68, 69.2, 69.3, 70, 71, 75.1, 86, 87, 88.2(b), 89(c), B5, F preamble, F, M1, *rule*
national authority and rule changes: 86.1(a), 86.2
navigable water: 18.1(a), 19.2, *mark*
normal position: B2.2, C2.1, *clear astern* and *clear ahead*, finish
not racing and rules (See *racing, not*)
notice board: 88.2(c), M1.6
notice of race: 70.4, 87.2, C preamble, F2.2(c), G3, J1, rule
notice to competitors: Race Signals
number of races, scoring: A1

Observer(s): 67, D preamble, D2.3, E3.1, N1
obstruction: 18 preamble, 18, 19, C2.6, E4.9, *two-length zone*
Offshore Racing Council (ORC): 76.2
Olympic Movement Anti-Doping Code: 5, Appendix 3
ooching: 42.2(c)
opposite *tack* (See *tack*, opposite)
ORC (Offshore Racing Council): 76.2
organizing authority: 63.7, 69.1(e), 75.1, 76.1, 87.2, 88.1, 89, D5, L2, M1.1, M2
organizing authority, duties of: 85, 87
outrigger: 50.3
outside boat: 18 preamble, 18.2

outside help: 1.1, 21, 41, 42.3(c), 47.2, D1.1(e), E4.2
overlap, overlapped: 11, 17.1, 18.2, 18.3(b), 18.4, 18.5, C2.6, *keep clear, leeward* and *windward*
overlap, broken: 18.2(b)
overlap, reasonable doubt: 18.2(e)
overlapped, not: 12, 18.2(c)
owner (See boat owner)

Party to a hearing: 61.1(c), 63, 64.1(a), 65, 66, C9.1, F2.2(e), F4, M1.4(b)
party to a hearing and appeal: 70.1, 71.3, 71.4, F6
penalized boat and scoring: 30.2, 44.1, 44.3
penalty: Sportsmanship and the Rules, 2, 30, 31.2, 44, 64.1, C7.2, G4, *finish, party*
penalty, acceptance of: 3(b)
penalty, cancelled: C2.1, C7.2(d)(e), C7.3(d), N3
penalty, informing of, reporting: 65.1, 69.1(c), 69.2(c), 69.3, 71.4
penalty, limits on: 44.4, C7.3
penalty, no: Part 2 preamble, 14(b), 36, 64.3(a), C5(a), D1.2(a), D2.2(b)
penalty, scoring: 30.2, 44.1, 44.3
penalty, starting: 30, E3.6
penalty, taking and completing: Sportsmanship and the Rules, C2.1, C2.2, C7.2(a), C7.4(a)
penalty, umpired event: C8
penalty and exoneration: 64.1, C8.1(b), E.5.8
penalty and fair sailing rule: 2
penalty and measurement: 64.3(a), 64.3(c), 65.3
penalty and *party* to a hearing: 71.3
penalty and rule 69: 69.1
penalty and rules of Part 2: 44
penalty signals: C5
penalty turns: 20, 22.2, 31.2, 44.1, 44.2, B4.3, C2.8, C2.10, C7.2(a), D2.1(b), D2.2(c)(d), E4.4, E5.8, N2.1
penalty turns (720°): 44.1, 44.2, N2.1
penalty without hearing: 30.2, 30.3, 63.1, 67, A5, N2
personal buoyancy: Race Signals, 1.2, 27.1, 40, E1.4
photographic evidence: L7
planing: 42.3(b)
port *tack* boat keeping clear: 10, 16.2
positive buoyancy, harness: 43.1(b)
postpone: Race Signals, 27.3, C3.2(d)(e), *racing*
postponed race and penalty rule: 30.2, 30.3, N3
precedence when rules conflict: Introduction, Part 2 Section C preamble, C8.1(b)
preparatory signal: Race Signals, 26, 27.2, 30, 45, 47.1, C3.1, C4, E3.5, E4.5, *racing*
prescriptions: Introduction, 68, 86, 88.2(b), F–H–M preambles, rule
prescriptions and changes to appendices: F–H–M preambles
prescriptions in sailing instructions, notice of race: 88.2(b), J2.2(5)(6)
prizes: A7, C11.3(c)
prohibited actions, propulsion: 42.2, E4.3

proper course: 17.2, 18.1(b), 18.4, C2.2, C2.10, D1.1(a)(c)
propulsion: 42, 42.3(c), B4.1, E4.3
propulsion (42) and penalty without hearing: 67, N2
protest (noun): 60–71
protest, informing
protestee: 61.1, E5.2, L1
protest, intending to: D2
protest, measurement: 43.1(c), 64.3, 65.3, 78.3, L2
protest, no right to: 60.1(a), C6.2
protest, not grounds for: 5
protest, right to: 60, C6.1, E5
protest, time limit (See time limit, *protest*)
protest, validity of: 60.2(a), 60.3(a), 61.1(c), 63.5, 71.2
protest, withdrawing: 63.1
protest between boats in different races: 63.7, L2
protest by protest or race committee: 43.1(c), 60.2(a), 60.3(a), 60.4, 61.1(b)(c), 78.3, N2.3
protest committee, appointment, duties, rights of: 60.3, 63.6, 85, 89, L preamble, *abandon, interested party, protest*
protest committee, recommendations for: L
protest committee and appeals: 70, 71
protest committee and rule 42: N1
protest committee decisions (See hearings and decisions)
protest committee request for confirmation, correction of decision: 70.2, F1, F2.3
protest contents: 61.2
protest form (See Contents page)
protestee, protestor: 61.1, 61.2(c)(d), 63.1, L3.2, *party* (See also *party* to a hearing)
protests, redress, hearings, misconduct and appeals: 60–71, L
pumping: 42.2(a)

Qualification to race: 75, B5

Race, conduct of: 25–36, 88.1
race, decision to: 4
race, entry and qualifications: 75–80
race, intention to: Part 2 preamble
race, rescheduled: 80
race committee: Introduction, Race Signals, *abandon, mark, party, protest, racing*
race committee, appointment of, responsibilities: 87.2, 88, 89
race committee, improper action or omission by, and redress: 62.1(a)
race committee and rule 42: N3
race committee and rule 69: 60.2(c), 69.1(e)
race committee right to protest, appeal: 43.1(c), 60.2, 70.1(b)
race office, delivery of *protests* to: 61.3, 63.1
race officials, appointment of: 87.2, 89(c), M1
race signals: Race Signals, 25–36, C3, E1.2, E3.5, *rule*
racing, Introduction, 4, Part 2 preamble, 22.1, 31.1, 44.1, 61.1(a), 62.1(b), 64.1(c), B4, C2.9, C4.1, C7.2(b), D2.1(b), D5.1, E3.1, E3.2, E3.3, E4.2(a)(b), E5.5, N1, *obstruction*
racing, not: Part 2 preamble, 22.1, 62.1(b), 64.1(c), C2.9, E3.3, E4.2(b), E5.5

racing area: Part 2 preamble, 61.1, E5.2
racing without certificate: 78.2
radio-controlled boat racing rules: E
recall: Race Signals, 26, *racing*
recall, general: 29.3, 30.3, E3.9, N3, *racing*
recall, individual: 29.2, E3.8
recover, recovering: B2.2, E4.5(b)
red flag: 61.1(a), C5(c), C6.3, C7.2(e), C6.1(b), C6.4(b), C7.3(d), D2.1(a)(c)(d), D2.2(b)(d), L3.1
red flag, breakdown: D5.1
red flag, no: 61.1(a), 62.2
red flag, redress: C6.3, C6.4(b)
redress, appeal: F2.2(a)
redress, hearings and decisions: 63.1, 64.2, 65.1, L3.4
redress, no: C9, D1.2(b), D2.2(h)
redress, requesting: 62, C6.3, C9.2, D2.2(h), E5.5, L3.2, *party*
redress, requirements for: 62, C6.4
redress, scoring: 64.2, A6, A10
redress, time limits: 62.2
repairs: 45, E5.9
representative: 61.2(d), 63.3(a), L2
resail, restart: 30.2, 30.3, 36, C6.6(b), D5.2, *abandon*
rescheduled races: 30.2, 30.3, 80
rescue, rescuing: 21
responsibility, personal: 1.2, 4, E1.4
retire: Sportsmanship and the Rules, 31.2, 44.1, 44.4(b), A5, A6, A9, C6.3, C10.2, D2.2, E4.9, E5.4, *racing*
right of way: Part 2 Section A
right of way, acquiring: 15
right of way and avoiding contact: 14
right-of-way boat: Part 2 Section A preamble, 16.1, 18.2(a), 18.4
rocking, rolling: 42.2(b), 42.3(a)
room: 14, 15, 16, 18 preamble, 18.2, 18.3(b), 18.5, *obstruction*
room, hail for: 19.1
room, not entitled to: 18.2(b)(c), 18.5
room to *tack* or gybe: 18 preamble, 19, C2.7
round-an-end rule, starting penalty: Race Signals, 20, 27.2, 29.2, 30.1, *start*
round-robin series: C10, C11
rounding a *mark*: 18
rule: Sportsmanship and the Rules, 3, 36, 64.1, 65.1, 68, 69.2, 70.1, 70.3, 71.3, 78.2, 85, 88.1, C2.11, C6.6, C8.1, C8.3, C8.4, C10.4, D1.1, D2.2, D3.1, D5.3, F1, F2.1, F3, J1.1, J1.2, L introduction, L3.2, J4, L5.3, *protest, rule*
rule 42, immediate penalties for breaking: N
rule interpretation, request for: 70.3, F1, F2.3
rules, breaking (See breach), *protest*
rules, changes to: Introduction, 86, 88.2(b), B–C–D–E–F preambles, G5, Appendices Section II preamble
rules, conflicting: Introduction, Part 2 Section A and Section C preambles
rules, testing proposed: 86.2

Safety: 1, 19.1, 21, 32.1(e), 40, 42.3(c), 48, J2.2(13)
sail, changing, setting and sheeting: 50, 54
sail, reef: 45, E4.5(c)

sail identification, numbers, advertising: 77, B7, E6, G, appendix 1
sail measurements: G1.1
sail substitutions: M2.2(b)
sailboard racing rules: B
sailing instructions: Introduction, Part 2 preamble, 88.2, J1, K, *mark*, *obstruction*, *rule*
sailing instructions, changes to: 25, 88.2(c), M2.3
sailing instructions and rule changes: Introduction, Part 2 preamble, 86.1(b)
sailing instructions and scoring: A1, A2
Sailing Instructions Guide: Appendix K
same *tack* (See *tack*, same)
scoring: 88.3, A, C10, D3, D4
scoring, abbreviations: A11
scoring, redress: 64.2, A6, A10
scoring, team racing: D3, D4, D5
scoring, ties: A7, A8, C11, D3.1(c), D4.2, D4.3
scoring and excluded races: 2, 30.3, 67, 88.3(b), A2
scoring and time limit: 35
scoring penalty: 30.2, 44.1, 44.3
scoring systems (Bonus Point, Low Point): A4
sculling: 42.2(d)
seamanship: 42.1, *room*
720° turns (See penalty turns, 720°)
sheet: 42.3(b), 50.3(a)
short course: 27.1
shortening the course: Race Signals, 32, 33, E3.10
signals, attention: C3.2(d)(e)
signals, arm: C2.7
signals, sound, failure of: 26, C3.1
signals, verbal: E3.5
signals, visual and sound: Race Signals, 25, 26, C3.1, C3.2(b), C5(f), E3.5, E3.9, N1
signals by umpires: C5
spinnaker: 50.4, C7.3
spinnaker pole: 50.2, 50.3(b)(2)
spinnaker staysail: 54
sportsmanship: Sportsmanship and the Rules, 2, 69.1(a), 69.2(a), C8.3(c), D2.2(d)
stability, changing: 51
standing rigging: 52
starboard-tack boat: 10, 16.2
start: 18.1(a), 19.2, 28.1, 29.1, 31.1, *postpone*
start, before the: Race Signals, 27, 76.1, C4, E3.5
start, did not: C8.5, D3.3
start, new: 29.3, 36, E3.9
(See resail, restart)
starting area: Race Signals, A9, A11
starting errors: 20, 29.3
starting line: 20, 28, 29, 30, B2.2, C3.2, E3.7, *mark*, *start*
starting *mark*: 18.1(a), 19.2, 27.2, 28.2, 31.1
starting mark, holding: B3
starting mark, moving: 27.2
starting races: 26
starting penalties: 30
starting procedure, error in: 29.3, 32.1(a)
starting signal(s), systems: Race Signals, 16.2, 20, 25-30, A3, C3.1, C3.2, E3.5, E3.9, *proper course*, *start*
string representing wake (sailing the course): 28.1
surfing: 42.3(b)
swim: 47.2

Tack (noun): *clear astern* and *clear ahead*, *keep clear*, *leeward* and *windward*
tack, opposite: 10, 16.2, 18.1(b), 18.3, C2.3, C2.6, *clear astern* and *clear ahead*; *overlap*
tack, room to: 19, C2.7
tack, same: 11, 12, 17.1, 19.1, *keep clear*, *leeward* and *windward*
tack, *starboard* or *port*: 10
tack, *tacking*: 13, 18 preamble, 18.3, 19.1
tacking and propulsion: 42.2(e), 42.3(a)
team racing rules: D
360° turns (See penalty turns)
ties, scoring (See scoring, ties)
time limit, appeals: F2.1, F6
time limit, extensions: 61.3, 62.2, L3.1
time limit, finish: 32.1(c), 35
time limit, in request for *protest* decision: 65.2
time limit, in request for redress: 62.2, C6.3, E5.5(b)
time limit, posting sailing instructions: 88.2(c)
time limit, *protest*: 44.3(a), 61.1(b), 61.3, E5.3, M1.4
time limit, race: 32.1(c), 35
time limit, reopening a hearing: 66, E5.10, F2.1
time to respond: 19.1
touching, holding a *mark*: 31, 44.4(a), B3
trapeze harness: 43.1(b)
tribunal or court: 3(c)
trim: 42.1, 50.1, 51
turns (See penalty turns)
20% starting penalty rule: Race Signals, 30.2, 36, 63.1, A4.2, A5, A11, E3.6
two-length zone: 18.2(b)(c), 18.3, C2.6

Umpire, umpire decisions: 87.2, C preamble, C6.5, C6.6, C7.2(b), D preamble, D2.2 upholding decision: 71.2

Validity of measurement or rating certificate: 78
validity of *protest*: 60.2(a), 60.3(a), 61.1(c), 63.5, 71.2, C6.4(b), L3.1

Warning signal: Race Signals, 26, 27.1, 29.3, 40, 88.2(c), C3.1, E3.5, E3.9
water tanks: 51
waterstarting: B1
weight of, weighing clothing and equipment: 43.1, H
wet suit: 40
whisker pole: 50.2, 50.3(b)(2)
wind and propulsion: 42.1, 42.2(e), 42.3(b)
windward, beat to: 17.2, 18.1(b), 42.3(b), D1.1(a)
windward boat: 11, 17.1, *keep clear*
witness: 60.1(a), 63.3(a), 63.4, 63.6, L3.1, L3.2

Zone (See *two-length zone*, four-length zone)

DEFINITIONS

A term used as stated below is shown in italic type or, in preambles, in bold italic type.

Abandon A race that a race committee or protest committee abandons is void but may be resailed.

Clear Astern and Clear Ahead; Overlap One boat is *clear astern* of another when her hull and equipment in normal position are behind a line abeam from the aftermost point of the other boat's hull and equipment in normal position. The other boat is *clear ahead*. They *overlap* when neither is *clear astern* or when a boat between them *overlaps* both. These terms do not apply to boats on opposite *tacks* unless rule 18 applies.

Finish A boat *finishes* when any part of her hull, or crew or equipment in normal position, crosses the finishing line in the direction of the course from the last *mark*, either for the first time or after taking a penalty under rule 31.2 or 44.2 or, under rule 28.1, after correcting an error made at the finishing line.

Interested Party A person who may gain or lose as a result of a protest committee's decision, or who has a close personal interest in the decision.

Keep Clear One boat *keeps clear* of another if the other can sail her course with no need to take avoiding action and, when the boats are *overlapped* on the same *tack*, if the *leeward* boat can change course in both directions without immediately making contact with the *windward* boat.

Leeward and Windward A boat's *leeward* side is the side that is to, or when she is head to wind, was away from the wind. However, when sailing by the lee or directly downwind, her leeward side is the side on which her mainsail lies. The other side is her *windward* side. When two boats on the same *tack* overlap, the one on the *leeward* side of the other is the *leeward* boat. The other is the *windward* boat.

Mark An object the sailing instructions require a boat to leave on a specified side, and a race committee vessel surrounded by navigable water from which the starting or finishing line extends. An anchor line and objects attached temporarily or accidentally to a *mark* are not part of it.

Obstruction An object that a boat could not pass without changing course substantially, if she were sailing directly towards it and one of her hull lengths from it. An object that can be safely passed on only one side and an area so designated by the sailing instructions are also *obstructions*. However, a boat *racing* is not an *obstruction* to other boats unless they are required to *keep clear* of her, give her *room* or, if rule 21 applies, avoid her.

Overlap See *Clear Astern* and *Clear Ahead*; *Overlap*.

Party A *party* to a hearing: a protestor; a protestee; a boat requesting redress; a boat or a competitor that may be penalized under rule 69.1; a race committee in a hearing under rule 62.1(a).

Postpone A *postponed* race is delayed before its scheduled start but may be started or *abandoned* later.

Proper Course A course a boat would sail to *finish* as soon as possible in the absence of the other boats referred to in the rule using the term. A boat has no *proper course* before her *starting* signal.

Protest An allegation made under rule 61.2 by a boat, a race committee or a protest committee that a boat has broken a *rule*.

Racing A boat is *racing* from her preparatory signal until she *finishes* and clears the finishing line and *marks* or retires, or until the race committee signals a general recall, *postponement* or *abandonment*.

Room The space a boat needs in the existing conditions while manoeuvring promptly in a seamanlike way.

Rule (a) The rules in this book, including the Definitions, Race Signals, Introduction, preambles and the rules of relevant appendices, but not titles;

(b) the prescriptions of the national authority, unless the sailing instructions state that they do not apply;

(c) the class rules, or the rules of the handicapping or rating system, except any that conflict with the rules in this book;

(d) the notice of race;

(e) the sailing instructions; and

(f) any other documents that govern the event.

Start A boat *starts* when after her starting signal any part of her hull, crew or equipment first crosses the starting line and she has complied with rule 29.1 and rule 30.1 if it applies.

Tack, Starboard or Port A boat is on the *tack*, *starboard* or *port*, corresponding to her windward side.

Two-Length Zone The area around a *mark* or *obstruction* within a distance of two hull lengths of the boat nearer to it.

Windward See *Leeward* and *Windward*.

RACE SIGNALS

The meanings of visual and sound signals are stated below. An arrow pointing up or down (▲▼) means that a visual signal is displayed or removed. A dot (•) means a sound; dots with dashes (• - - - •) mean repetitive sounds. When a visual signal is displayed over a class flag, the signal applies only to that class.

COLOUR CODE
Blue   Red   Yellow

Postponement Signals

AP Races not started are *postponed*. The warning signal will be made 1 minute after removal unless at that time the race is *postponed* again or *abandoned*.
▲ • • ▼ •

AP over H
Races not started are *postponed*. Further signals ashore.
▲ • •

AP over A
Races not started are *postponed*. No more racing today.
▲ • •

Penant 1 ▲ • • ▼ •

Penant 2 ▲ • • ▼ •

Penant 3 ▲ • • ▼ •

Penant 4 ▲ • • ▼ •

Penant 5 ▲ • • ▼ •

Penant 6 ▲ • • ▼ •

A-P over a numeral pennant 1-6 *Postponement* of 1-6 hours from the scheduled startig time

Abandonment Signals

N All races that have started are *abandoned*. Return to the starting area. The warning signal will be made 1 minute after removal unless at that time the race is *abandoned* again or *postponed*.
▲ • • • • ▼ •

N over H All races are *abandoned*. Further signals ashore.
▲ • • •

N over A All races are *abandoned*. No more racing today.
▲ • • •

Recall Signals

X Individual recall.
▲ •

First Substitute
General recall. The warning signal will be made 1 minute after removal.
• - - - •

Signals before the Start

P Preparatory signal.
▲ • ▼ •

I Rule 30.1 is in effect.
▲ • ▼ •

Z Rule 30.2 is in effect.
▲ • ▼ •

Black flag. Rule 30.3 is in effect.
▲ • ▼ •

Course Change

S No later than the warning signal: Sail the short course. At a rounding or finishing *mark*: *Finish* between the nearby *mark* and the staff displaying this flag.
▲ • •

C The position of the next *mark* has been changed
• - - - •

Other Signals

L Ashore: A notice to competitors has been posted. Afloat: Come within hail or follow this boat.
▲ •

M The object displaying this signal replaces a missing *mark*.
• - - - •

Y Wear personal buoyancy.
▲ •

(no sound)
Blue flag or shape. This race committee boat is in position at the finishing line.

"As sailors, we can always count on volunteer lifeboat crews. Can they count on you? Please join *Offshore* today."

Sir Robin Knox-Johnston CBE, RD*

However experienced you are at sea, you never know when you'll need the help of a lifeboat crew. But to keep saving lives, the Royal National Lifeboat Institution's volunteer crews need *your* help.

That is why you should join **Offshore**. For just £3.50 per month, you can help save thousands of lives, receive practical information to help keep *you* safe at sea *and* save money on equipment for your boat. *Please join us today.*

Please join *Offshore* – today

Please photocopy and return this form, with your payment if appropriate, to: RNLI, FREEPOST, West Quay Road, Poole, Dorset BH15 1XF.

Mr/Mrs/Miss/Ms ☐ Initial ☐ Surname ☐

Address ☐

Postcode ☐

I would like to join:

☐ **As an *Offshore* member at £** ☐ per month/quarter/year * (min £3.50 per month/£10 per quarter/£40 per year)

☐ **As Joint *Offshore* members at £** ☐ per month/quarter/year *

(Husband & Wife, min £6 per month/£17.50 per quarter/£70 per year) * please delete as applicable

Please debit the above sum as indicated from my Visa/MasterCard * now and at the prevailing rate until cancelled by me in writing.

Card No. ☐☐☐☐ ☐☐☐☐ ☐☐☐☐ ☐☐☐☐ Expiry date ☐ /

Signature ☐

(Please give address of cardholder on a separate piece of paper if different from above.)

Alternatively, I wish to pay my **Offshore** membership by cheque/PO

I enclose a cheque/Postal Order for **£** ☐ payable to Royal National Lifeboat Institution.

Or, I wish to pay my subscription by Direct Debit ☐

Please tick the box – a Direct Debit form will be sent to you.   FERN10

Lifeboats
Offshore

Because life's not all plain sailing

Registered Charity No. 209603